AF578037

The Boy Who Crossed the World with Marco Polo

Fayzullakhuja Uktamboev

Published by Uktamboev Press, 2024.

While every precaution has been taken in the preparation of this book, the publisher assumes no responsibility for errors or omissions, or for damages resulting from the use of the information contained herein.

THE BOY WHO CROSSED THE WORLD WITH MARCO POLO

First edition. December 5, 2024.

Copyright © 2024 Fayzullakhuja Uktamboev.

ISBN: 979-8230642022

Written by Fayzullakhuja Uktamboev.

Table of Contents

Travel is a great Idea

The Boy Who Crossed the World with Marco Polo

Table of Contents

Introduction

About the Author: Uktamboev Fayzullakhuja

Greetings, dear reader!

My name is **Uktamboev Fayzullakhuja**, and I come from the vibrant and culturally rich land of **Uzbekistan**, located in Central Asia. Growing up, I was surrounded by the whispers of ancient cities like Samarkand and Bukhara, once bustling with traders, scholars, and adventurers. It was in this unique environment that I first encountered stories of explorers, conquerors, and those who dared to dream beyond the horizons. These tales, passed down through generations, have always inspired me and filled me with a sense of wonder about the world.

One such story that never left my mind was that of **Marco Polo**, the Venetian merchant who ventured far beyond the known world to reach the court of **Kublai Khan** in China. His tales, documented in *The Travels of Marco Polo*, opened my eyes to the incredible possibilities of exploration and adventure. As I grew older, I began to wonder: *What would it have been like to travel with Marco Polo?* And so, this book was born.

The journey of **Thomas Polo**, the young boy who crosses the world with Marco Polo, mirrors not just the historical adventure of an incredible explorer, but also the personal journey we all take in our lives. In this story, I hope to remind you that every journey begins with a single step. Sometimes that step is fueled by curiosity, and other times it's driven by a deep desire to discover who we truly are. No matter the road we walk, the adventures we embark on shape us, mold us, and reveal parts of ourselves we never knew existed.

This story is for anyone who has ever dreamed of crossing vast oceans, walking through bustling markets, or gazing at the stars in a distant land. It is for those who believe that the world is full of wonders waiting to be discovered. But most of all, this story is for you—because every reader has their own journey, and I hope this book inspires you to take that first step into the unknown.

Chapter 1: A Life by the Docks

The city of Venice stood at the crossroads of the world. Its canals shimmered like veins of silver under the morning sun, reflecting the bustling life of a city that had, for centuries, drawn travelers, traders, and adventurers from across the known world.

Thomas Polo, though still young, could already feel the rhythm of Venice in his bones. The lapping of the water against the stone piers, the calls of sailors and merchants hawking their goods, the steady creak of wooden ships bobbing in the harbor—all these sounds were as familiar to him as the voice of his father, Antonio, calling him from the workshop.

"Thomas!" Antonio's voice cut through the noise, sharp and commanding, like the sound of a ship's bell ringing at dawn. "Get over here. The mast's not going to raise itself."

Thomas sighed and wiped his hands on his trousers. His father's shipyard was a busy place, a maze of ropes, pulleys, and wooden beams, where the ships that would sail across the Mediterranean were built with care and precision. Antonio Polo had spent most of his life here, crafting the sturdy vessels that carried Venetian traders to distant lands. The ships were the lifeblood of the city, and Antonio had made his living off them.

But for Thomas, the docks felt like a cage.

He stood on the edge of the pier, looking out over the water, his mind drifting away from the work at hand. He often wondered what lay beyond the horizon. The great cities of the East, the markets of Alexandria, the deserts of Persia, the vast lands of China—it was all so far from Venice, so out of reach. Yet every time he heard the stories, the dreams of those who had seen the world, his heart raced with longing.

His father's footsteps were heavy on the wooden planks as he approached, the leather of his boots creaking with each step.

"You're not going to stand there all day, are you?" Antonio grumbled. "The ship's waiting for the last touches before we can sail her out."

Thomas turned reluctantly. His father's broad shoulders and weathered face were framed by the towering masts of the ship, a symbol of the life Thomas was expected to follow. He respected his father—Antonio was a master shipbuilder, after all—but Thomas could not bring himself to love this life.

"I was just thinking about something," Thomas said quietly, avoiding his father's sharp gaze.

"Thinking?" Antonio snorted, clearly unimpressed. "The only thing you should be thinking about is how to get that mast in place. No time for daydreaming, boy."

Thomas's heart tightened, a familiar ache settling in his chest. His father had always been a man of action, practical, grounded. Antonio believed in hard work and solid results—traits that made him successful but also made him blind to anything beyond the world of ships and trade.

But Thomas had always known there was more. He had heard stories from the old sailors who gathered in the marketplaces, telling tales of far-off lands where the streets were lined with gold, where strange spices filled the air, and where emperors rode on horses taller than any he'd ever seen. Marco Polo, the famous Venetian traveler, had been to all these places. Marco Polo had seen what Thomas could only dream of.

It was a dream he couldn't let go of, no matter how much his father tried to push him into the family business.

"Father," Thomas began, his voice barely above a whisper, "have you ever thought about traveling? I mean, really traveling, like Marco Polo did. To the East, to China..."

Antonio's eyes hardened, and he shook his head slowly. "Don't be foolish, Thomas. The world is here. The work is here. You want to waste your time chasing shadows? I've built a life for us here, and I expect you to take up the mantle. This ship, this city, that's your future."

Thomas's heart sank. He knew the conversation would go this way. He had tried before, mentioning his longing to see the world, to follow in the footsteps of the great explorers. But Antonio was always quick to dismiss it, as if the world beyond the Venetian docks was a place for dreamers, not men of action.

"I'm just saying..." Thomas hesitated, his mind racing for the right words. But before he could speak again, a loud voice cut through the air.

"Ah, young Thomas! I've got a story for you, lad. Come listen!" The voice belonged to one of the old sailors who had seen more of the world than most people in Venice ever would.

Thomas turned and saw the old man, his weathered face lined with years of travel, standing at the edge of the dock with a knowing grin.

"You'll be telling him more stories, Vito?" Antonio grumbled, clearly annoyed at the interruption.

Vito's eyes twinkled mischievously. "Not just stories, my friend—tales of adventure. Stories that will make this boy's heart long for the sea and the distant lands. Come here, lad," he called to Thomas. "I'll tell you of a place where the sun never sets and the mountains are as high as the sky."

Thomas's heart quickened. His father's frown deepened, but Thomas didn't care. This was what he lived for—the stories, the dreams, the vision of a world far bigger than the docks of Venice.

With a final, lingering glance at his father, Thomas hurried toward Vito. As he walked away, he felt a stirring inside him, a whisper of something greater, something that might just be within reach if he could find the courage to take that first step.

Certainly! Let's continue with the next section of the book, where Thomas is introduced to more of the world beyond Venice, and his dreams start to take shape through the stories of the sailors and adventurers he meets.

Chapter 2: The Stories of Marco Polo

Thomas settled beside Vito, eager to hear the old sailor's tales. The sun was setting over the Grand Canal, casting long shadows across the docks as the distant clink of metal and chatter of sailors filled the evening air. The scent of saltwater mixed with the faint traces of fish, spices, and the rich aroma of fresh bread from a nearby bakery.

Vito sat down on a worn crate, a twinkle in his eye. He had lived many years, and the stories he told weren't just words—they were memories, woven into the fabric of his life.

"Ah, young Thomas," Vito began, his voice low and raspy. "You've heard the name, haven't you? Marco Polo. A Venetian like yourself. But he wasn't like the others. He didn't stay in Venice his whole life. Oh no, he ventured far beyond the canals, beyond the shores of this city, and into lands that most of us will never see. He saw the world, lad. The real world."

Thomas leaned forward, his heart racing. Marco Polo—he had heard his name spoken in hushed tones at the marketplace, whispered in reverence by sailors and traders who came back from the East. But hearing the stories from someone who had known the man's legacy, someone who had lived through the same trade routes, brought the adventure to life in ways that made Thomas's chest swell with longing.

"He traveled to places," Vito continued, his weathered hand tracing the outline of a distant horizon, "where the mountains reached up to the sky, where the deserts stretched so far you thought you might fall off the earth, and where cities glittered like jewels in the sand. The places Marco Polo visited weren't just cities—they were kingdoms, each more exotic and wondrous than the last."

Thomas's eyes widened, his imagination running wild. He could almost see it—grand palaces, bustling markets, the golden spires of unknown empires rising from the mist. Marco Polo had touched them all, and here he was, in Venice, just a few generations removed from this great journey. It felt as though a door had opened to a world that Thomas had always imagined, a world where his dreams could come true.

Vito leaned closer, his voice dropping to a whisper, as if he were about to reveal a secret. "Marco Polo didn't just visit these places, Thomas. He lived them. He met emperors, princes, and monks. He crossed deserts on camelback, sailed across vast oceans, and found riches beyond what any man could imagine. And the stories he brought back to Venice? Well, they changed the way the world saw the East. People didn't know what lay beyond those lands, but Marco Polo told them."

Thomas sat back, his mind spinning. His gaze was distant, focused not on the old sailor in front of him, but on the endless horizon beyond the Venetian docks. For the first time, he could see it all clearly. It wasn't just about leaving Venice; it was about finding something greater, something that was calling him beyond his father's expectations.

Vito chuckled, noticing the faraway look in Thomas's eyes. "You've got the fire in you, lad. I can see it. I had that fire when I was young, too. But Marco Polo didn't just follow his dreams—he fought for them. His journey wasn't easy. There were dangers everywhere. Bandits, storms, and even betrayal. It was the hardest journey a man could take. But Marco Polo, he wasn't afraid of those dangers. He knew that the greatest treasures in life aren't the ones you can touch with your hands—they're the ones that live in your heart. The knowledge, the wisdom, the adventures you can only find by stepping into the unknown."

Thomas felt a stirring inside him, a pull so strong it seemed to come from deep within his chest. He had always thought about the world beyond Venice, but now it felt like a calling. A need to leave everything he knew and find out what lay on the other side. To see for himself the lands Marco Polo had spoken of, to walk the paths of emperors and adventurers. He could feel the weight of it already—the call to adventure was too strong to ignore.

"How did Marco Polo manage it?" Thomas asked, almost to himself.

Vito smiled knowingly. "He didn't do it alone. He had his family, his father and uncle, who were traders. They knew the way, knew the routes, and took Marco with them when he was just a boy like you. But even when they got to the court of Kublai Khan, Marco Polo didn't stop. He learned languages, made alliances, and helped the Mongol Empire in ways no one could have imagined. He became someone important—not because he was wealthy or powerful, but because he understood the world in a way no one else did."

Thomas could feel his pulse quicken as Vito's words sank in. He was no longer just a boy from Venice. He was someone destined for something greater. The world was out there, just waiting to be explored, and all he had to do was take that first step.

"But the most important lesson Marco Polo taught," Vito said with a finality in his voice, "is that it's not enough to dream. You have to make those dreams real. And if you don't follow them, lad, no one else will."

Thomas swallowed, a lump forming in his throat. He looked back at the docks where his father stood, watching them from a distance. The weight of Antonio Polo's expectations hung heavy on his shoulders. Thomas knew the life his father wanted for him—a life of shipbuilding, of routine, of safety—but the world outside Venice called to him like a siren's song.

"I think I understand," Thomas whispered. His voice trembled, not from fear, but from the enormity of the decision he was about to make.

Vito clapped him on the back with a hearty laugh. "You've got it, lad. You've got it."

As the old sailor continued his tale, Thomas's mind raced. The sun had dipped low, casting the city in soft, golden light, but in his heart, a fire burned bright. Tomorrow, he would speak to his father. Tomorrow, he would leave Venice. It was time to follow in Marco Polo's footsteps, to see the world for himself, to turn his dreams into reality.

Chapter 3: The Turning Point

The next few days felt like a haze to Thomas. Vito's words echoed in his mind, stirring something deep inside him. He could no longer ignore the yearning that had been building for years—the longing to see the world beyond the Venetian canals. But now, reality began to settle in.

His father, Antonio Polo, had noticed his son's distant mood. The stern shipbuilder had been working late into the night, but each time he passed the house, he would glance at Thomas, who would look away. Antonio had never been one for unnecessary displays of affection, but he could tell something was different about his son. The air between them had shifted, a quiet tension hanging in their home.

One evening, as the golden light of sunset bathed the room in a warm glow, Antonio sat down at the dining table. His broad shoulders seemed to fill the space, and his thick, weathered hands grasped the edge of the table. His eyes, dark and serious, never left Thomas.

"You've been distracted lately, Thomas," his father said, his voice low and steady. "What's on your mind?"

Thomas swallowed, trying to muster the courage to speak the words that had been building inside him for so long. He had spent countless nights thinking about this moment, imagining how he would break the news, but now that the time had come, the words caught in his throat.

"I... I've been thinking," Thomas began, his voice faltering. "I want to go—go to the East. To follow Marco Polo's path. To see the world, father."

Antonio's eyes narrowed, and his face hardened. He leaned back in his chair, crossing his arms over his chest. "You want to leave Venice?" His voice was steady, but the surprise was evident in his eyes. "You think you can just sail away like that? You think the world is some grand adventure, like the stories you've heard? I've seen men like you—young, full of dreams—who think they can conquer the world. But the world doesn't care for your dreams, Thomas. It will break you."

Thomas's heart raced. His father's words were like cold water, but he refused to back down. "I'm not like those men," he said, standing up, his voice firm now. "I've learned from them, but I want to see for myself. I want to experience the world beyond Venice. I don't want to live in the shadow of others' dreams. I want to make my own."

Antonio slammed his fist on the table, and the loud noise reverberated through the room. "Your dream will get you killed. It's not like in the stories. I've spent my life building ships, teaching men the ways of the sea, so they don't end up lost or broken in some faraway land. You think Marco Polo's tales will keep you safe? They won't. The world is dangerous. You have no idea what you're asking for."

Thomas felt the words sting, but he stood his ground. "Maybe I don't know what I'm asking for. But I'll never know unless I try. You taught me to be strong, to work with my hands and build, but now I need to build something else. I need to build my own life. I need to know what's out there."

Antonio stared at him for a long time, his jaw clenched. There was a flicker of something in his eyes—maybe fear, maybe understanding, but it quickly faded behind his mask of authority.

"You are a fool if you think you can just leave like that," Antonio said, his voice cold. "If you go, you'll be on your own. Don't come crawling back when the world breaks you."

The words cut deep, but Thomas felt something within him harden, a resolve that made him stand taller than he ever had before. He could feel the weight of his father's disapproval pressing down on him, but it was nothing compared to the weight of his own dreams.

"I won't come back until I've seen the world," Thomas said quietly, his voice steady. He turned and walked toward the door, feeling the finality of his words settle into his bones. He knew what he had to do.

As Thomas stepped outside into the cool night air, the sounds of the city—of the waves lapping against the docks, of sailors calling out to each other—seemed to fill his ears. The city, his home, was still there, but it felt distant now. He could see it, but he could no longer be a part of it in the way his father expected. The world was calling him.

That night, as Thomas lay in bed, he held his grandfather's old map close to his chest. The faded parchment, filled with intricate lines and markings of distant lands, was like a treasure he couldn't keep to himself any longer. He traced the routes with his finger—the path Marco Polo had taken, the cities he'd visited, the vast lands that lay beyond Venice. The map seemed to pulse with possibility.

In the quiet darkness of his room, Thomas made a decision that would change his life forever. Tomorrow, he would leave Venice. He would leave behind his father's shipyard, his mother's worried glances, and the safe, familiar world he had always known. He would follow in the footsteps of Marco Polo.

Chapter 4: The Map and the Vision

The morning sun peeked over the rooftops of Venice, casting long shadows along the narrow streets of the city. The air was cool and smelled faintly of saltwater, the fragrance of the sea reaching Thomas's nose as he crept through the quiet streets. It was still early—too early for anyone to notice his departure. The city was just waking up, and most of the docks would be busy with the comings and goings of the ships in a few hours.

Thomas, however, had no intention of being seen. The decision he had made the night before burned within him, but so did the fear—the fear of what he was leaving behind, the fear of what he might lose, and the fear of how his father would react. But all of that seemed smaller now, almost insignificant in the face of the possibility that lay before him.

With his heart pounding in his chest, he made his way to the old wooden chest in the attic. It had belonged to his grandfather, a man who had sailed the seas in his youth and whose stories of adventure had sparked the fire in Thomas's heart long before he had even heard of Marco Polo. The chest was weathered, the brass latch worn with age, but the map inside was what Thomas had come to find.

The map was a tattered relic, yellowed with age, the edges curled and fragile. It had been passed down to him by his grandfather, who had once hoped Thomas might take up the same journey he had started decades ago, only to be stopped by time and circumstance. Now, it was Thomas's turn. He ran his fingers over the faded ink, tracing the winding paths that stretched across the world, from the bustling markets of Constantinople to the majestic cities of China. Each line represented a story—each dot a city he had dreamed of seeing.

The map was more than just a piece of paper; it was a vision. It was a key to a world beyond the horizon, a world full of mystery and wonder. Thomas could almost hear the distant call of the markets, the clattering of hooves on dirt roads, the rustle of silk in the wind. The world was out there, waiting for him, and he couldn't wait any longer.

He packed the essentials—his grandfather's map, some dried bread, a flask of water, and a small pouch of coins he had saved up. The sea was his destiny, and he was ready to face whatever challenges it would bring.

The journey to the docks felt like the longest of Thomas's life. His feet felt heavy, each step pulling him away from the only home he had ever known. The streets, once familiar, now seemed strange, as though they were filled with hidden meanings he had never noticed before. As he walked, his mind raced with thoughts of his father, his mother, and the life he was leaving behind. Would they understand? Would they forgive him?

But the thought of the East, of the adventure that awaited, kept him moving forward.

By the time he reached the docks, the first rays of sunlight were beginning to sparkle on the water's surface, the ships slowly stirring to life. He spotted the vessel he had been watching for days—a merchant ship bound for the East, its sails unfurled and ready to catch the wind. It was a small ship, nothing like the great galleons his father built, but it would carry him toward his dreams.

His heart beat faster as he approached the ship. The crew was busy unloading crates of goods, and no one seemed to notice him at first. Thomas took a deep breath and, using the skills he had learned watching his father's crew, he snuck aboard, slipping between the ropes and cargo, keeping to the shadows.

A few minutes later, he was aboard.

For a long moment, he stood there, hidden behind some crates, looking at the bustling port of Venice. The familiar sights—the towering buildings, the busy market squares—were beginning to fade as the ship gently pulled away from the dock. His chest tightened, and he could feel the weight of what he had just done. He was leaving everything behind. There would be no turning back now.

His breath caught in his throat as the ship left the harbor and began to make its way through the narrow canals, heading toward the open sea. A strange mixture of exhilaration and fear churned in his stomach. What had he done? He was following his dreams, but was he ready for what lay ahead?

He couldn't answer that yet. The horizon ahead of him, the endless expanse of the sea, seemed to promise something greater, something he couldn't quite grasp but could feel in his bones. This was the moment he had been waiting for. This was the beginning of his own story.

As the ship left Venice behind, Thomas climbed up the side to the deck, where the salty breeze tugged at his hair and filled his lungs. The crew was busy, none of them noticing the young boy who had snuck aboard. The captain, a tall man with dark hair and a sharp gaze, was giving orders to the sailors, his voice cutting through the wind.

Thomas stood on the deck, feeling the ship rock beneath him. The sea stretched out before him, vast and infinite. For the first time in his life, he felt truly free. He wasn't just a boy in Venice anymore. He was an adventurer, and the world was his to explore.

His heart soared as the ship moved further into the open sea. The sun climbed higher in the sky, casting its warm golden light on the vast expanse of water. He looked at the map in his hands, the path he would follow now clearly marked. The journey ahead would be difficult, no doubt. There would be storms, hunger, and challenges beyond his imagination. But none of that mattered now. Thomas Polo had made his choice, and the adventure of a lifetime had begun.

Chapter 5: The Secret Departure

The morning sun cast a fiery orange glow across the horizon as the ship sailed smoothly out of the Venetian Lagoon. The great city of Venice was now a mere silhouette on the horizon, its ornate buildings slowly shrinking as the ship advanced into the vast Mediterranean Sea. Thomas stood at the ship's bow, his hands gripping the wooden railing as the cool, salty breeze tugged at his hair. His heart pounded with excitement, the thrill of adventure filling every corner of his soul. He was free now—truly free.

The ship, a small but sturdy merchant vessel named *La Nuova Stella*, rocked gently as it made its way toward the open waters. Its sails were full, catching the wind that would carry them eastward. The ship's crew, mostly rough-hewn men with sun-beaten faces, moved with practiced efficiency, hauling ropes and adjusting sails. Thomas, who had spent years watching the men at work on his father's ships, felt a strange mix of pride and nervousness as he observed them. He was no longer an observer; he was one of them now.

The captain of the ship, a man named Giovanni, stood at the wheel, his weathered hands steady as he guided the ship through the waves. Giovanni was a man of few words, and Thomas quickly learned that he didn't have much interest in conversation, especially with a young boy. But Thomas didn't mind. He was content to observe, soaking in every bit of knowledge he could about the sea and its mysteries.

For the first few days, the ship sailed smoothly across the Mediterranean, making its way toward the southern shores of Greece. Thomas spent most of his time on the deck, watching the sailors, learning the ropes, and listening intently to their stories. There were tales of strange creatures in the deep, of vast storms that had swept entire fleets to the bottom of the sea, and of treasure lost to time.

The days were long, and the work was hard. The crew worked in shifts, hauling heavy cargo, mending sails, and cleaning the ship's decks. Thomas, eager to prove himself, threw himself into the tasks, carrying crates and assisting with the ropes. His muscles ached, and his body grew tired, but there was a strange sense of satisfaction in the work—something he had never felt in Venice.

In the evenings, after the sun dipped below the horizon and the stars appeared in the sky like scattered jewels, the crew would gather around a fire on deck. They would sing songs in languages Thomas had never heard, telling tales of distant lands and forgotten kingdoms. The salty air, the sound of the waves crashing against the hull, and the creaking of the ship under the weight of the ocean all blended together into a rhythm that made Thomas feel as though he was a part of something greater, something timeless.

On the fourth day, as the ship passed the coast of Greece and made its way toward the islands of the Aegean Sea, Thomas stood on the deck, watching the land fade into the distance. He had never been beyond the walls of Venice before. The Mediterranean, with its azure waters and endless horizon, was like a new world to him. The reality of his journey was beginning to sink in. There was no turning back now.

The crew had taken notice of Thomas's enthusiasm. Giovanni, who had initially kept his distance, now called him over to help with the navigation. With a gruff nod, the captain handed Thomas a small compass and pointed toward the horizon.

"Know the way by the stars, boy," Giovanni said, his voice low and rough. "The sea is vast, and it will try to deceive you. But the stars... the stars will always guide you home."

Thomas nodded, staring at the tiny compass in his hand. The instrument was simple—nothing more than a small needle floating in water—but to Thomas, it was a symbol of everything he had come for. This tiny device, a simple tool, would guide him across the unknown seas, leading him toward his destiny.

The days passed in a steady rhythm, and Thomas's knowledge of the ship grew. He learned how to read the winds, how to steer through narrow straits, and how to predict the weather by the patterns of the clouds. He discovered that life on the sea was not easy—there were no comforts like those in Venice, no familiar faces or warm hearths to return to at night. But there was something about the simplicity of it all, something raw and untamed, that filled Thomas with a sense of purpose.

One evening, as the ship neared the coast of Turkey, a strange tension filled the air. The crew had grown quieter, more alert. Giovanni stood at the helm, his eyes narrowed, scanning the horizon. The wind had shifted, and the waves were growing restless. Thomas joined him on the deck, watching the darkening sky.

"There's a storm brewing," Giovanni muttered, his voice barely audible over the howling wind. "We need to make port before it hits."

Thomas's heart skipped a beat. The sea, which had once seemed so vast and inviting, now felt like a beast ready to pounce. The horizon had darkened, the sky a swirling mass of gray clouds. Thomas could feel the change in the air—the tension of the crew, the tightening of the ropes, the urgency in Giovanni's voice.

"We'll make it," Giovanni said, though his eyes were grim. "But the sea has a way of testing you. It will take everything you have, and more."

As the ship sailed closer to the shore, the wind began to howl, and the first drops of rain started to fall. The crew scrambled to secure the sails and prepare for the storm. Thomas, his heart racing, worked alongside them, tying down ropes and holding onto the ship's rails as the waves began to crash higher and higher against the hull.

The storm hit with a fury unlike anything Thomas had ever experienced. The ship rocked violently, the sails flapping in the wind like a flag caught in a storm. The sky was dark, the waves towering over the ship, as if the very sea was trying to swallow them whole. Thomas had never felt so small, so insignificant, in the face of nature's power.

Yet, in the chaos of the storm, he also felt something else—something deep within himself that had been dormant. A sense of clarity, of understanding, washed over him. The sea was wild, unpredictable, and dangerous. But it was also beautiful, in its own terrifying way. And like Marco Polo before him, Thomas understood that to truly see the world, he had to face the storm. He had to embrace the challenges, the hardships, and the dangers.

The crew fought with everything they had, guiding the ship through the storm's fury. It seemed to last for hours, though Thomas couldn't be sure. But eventually, the storm passed, the winds died down, and the ship was calm again. The sun peeked through the clouds, casting a golden light on the water, and the ship sailed on.

Thomas stood at the bow, his hands gripping the railing, his chest still heaving from the effort. He was soaked to the bone, his face streaked with saltwater, but his eyes shone with a newfound determination. The world was out there, waiting for him. And he was ready.

Chapter 6: The First Sail

After the storm, the sea calmed as if it had been a mere tantrum, leaving the crew with nothing but a solemn sense of triumph. They had survived. But Thomas knew that the true test was not in surviving the storm but in enduring what lay ahead. The storm had only been the beginning. There were many more trials to come, each one shaping him, testing his resolve.

As the *La Nuova Stella* sailed toward the coast of Greece, the Mediterranean revealed its softer side. The turquoise waters, calm and inviting, shimmered under the golden rays of the sun. The distant shores of the Greek islands emerged from the mist, their whitewashed buildings perched on steep hillsides. For a moment, the ship felt like it was in a dream, as if the world was stretching out in front of him like an open book, each page a new adventure.

The first stop was the island of Crete, a place of ancient ruins and stories that had been passed down through generations. The island, known for its rich history and legendary labyrinths, was bustling with life as the ship docked at the port. Merchants lined the piers, their carts piled high with goods—spices, textiles, olive oil, and exotic fruits that Thomas had never seen before.

As Thomas stepped off the ship and onto the warm, sunlit docks, he was struck by the vibrancy of the island. The air was thick with the scent of fresh bread baking in nearby ovens and the tang of saltwater. People of all kinds bustled about—traders from the Levant, sailors from the farthest reaches of the Mediterranean, and local Cretans with their distinctive accents and wide-brimmed hats.

Giovanni, the captain, led Thomas and the crew into the heart of the bustling market. "Stay close," Giovanni warned, his voice low and watchful. "The island is full of travelers and merchants from all corners of the world. They're not all friendly."

Thomas nodded, his eyes wide with curiosity. He had read about the great markets of the East, where silk and spices flowed like rivers, but to see it with his own eyes was something else entirely. It was a maze of colors—bright red pomegranates, golden honey, and rich green olives—and the sounds were a cacophony of languages Thomas didn't recognize, from the guttural Turkish to the lilting Arabic. There was a rhythm here, a pulse that seemed to beat in time with the ocean itself.

He followed Giovanni through the market, dodging carts and people, until they reached a small stall at the edge of the market. The stall was run by an old woman who greeted them with a sharp, appraising look.

"A fine ship you have there," she said, her eyes twinkling. "But you're far from home, aren't you, young man?"

Thomas smiled nervously, unsure of how to respond. He had never been good at speaking with strangers, especially those with sharp eyes like this woman.

Giovanni, noticing the exchange, spoke up. "We're looking for supplies. The journey to the East is long, and we'll need to restock before we sail again."

The old woman nodded and moved behind her stall, rummaging through baskets filled with dried herbs and bundles of cloth. "I have just what you need," she said, her hands moving with surprising speed for her age. "But beware, traveler. The world is full of wonders, but also dangers. Keep your eyes open, and your heart even more so."

Thomas felt a shiver run down his spine at the old woman's words. She wasn't just talking about the sea, he realized. She was talking about the world. The vast, unknown world that lay beyond the horizon.

As the day passed, Thomas wandered through the streets of Crete, his mind racing with excitement. Everywhere he turned, there were new things to discover. A group of children playing with a ball in the street, their laughter echoing off the stone walls. A group of traders from Egypt, haggling over the price of fine linen. An old man sitting in a doorway, carving intricate patterns into a piece of wood with a steady hand.

Thomas felt like a stranger in this new world, but that sense of strangeness was quickly replaced by wonder. Everywhere he looked, he saw something unfamiliar, something he had never imagined. It was as if the world had opened up to him in a way he could never have anticipated.

When night fell, the market grew quieter, and the cool breeze off the sea brought a sense of calm. The crew gathered in a nearby tavern to rest, and Thomas joined them, still filled with the energy of the day's discoveries. As the sailors shared stories over mugs of wine, Giovanni leaned over to him.

"You've seen it, haven't you?" Giovanni asked. "The world. It's bigger than Venice, bigger than anything you ever dreamed."

Thomas nodded, his gaze distant. "I've seen more in one day than I ever thought possible."

Giovanni's eyes softened, and for the first time, Thomas saw a hint of approval in the captain's gaze. "The world is full of stories, boy. But it's up to you to find your own. And when you do, it will change you forever."

Thomas didn't fully understand the weight of Giovanni's words, but he felt them deep within him. The world was a vast, unknowable place, and each day was a new chapter in an adventure that had only just begun.

The next morning, as the ship set sail once again, leaving the island of Crete behind, Thomas stood at the bow, watching the island fade into the distance. The journey ahead was long, and the sea was unpredictable, but for the first time, Thomas felt certain of one thing—he was on the right path.

Chapter 7: The Mediterranean

As the *La Nuova Stella* glided through the calm Mediterranean waters, the sun dipped lower in the sky, bathing the sea in a warm, amber glow. Thomas stood at the ship's bow, his gaze fixed on the distant land ahead. The air, salt-tinged and heavy with the promise of adventure, filled his lungs as the wind played with his hair. In his heart, an unfamiliar mixture of excitement and uncertainty churned. They were approaching Constantinople—the legendary city that lay at the crossroads of two worlds. He had heard stories of its grandeur, its markets, and its culture, but seeing it with his own eyes was something entirely different.

As the land of Turkey slowly took shape on the horizon, Thomas found his thoughts adrift, wondering if he was truly ready for what lay ahead. He had sailed across the Mediterranean before, but this was different. This was Constantinople—where East met West, where Asia and Europe collided. A city so grand that it was said to be impossible to capture in one's imagination, no matter how vivid the stories.

The ship cut through the water, its sails filled with the winds that pushed them toward this new and unknown chapter of Thomas's journey. Soon, the first hints of the city began to emerge, like an illusion materializing from the haze of the sea. Towers and minarets, domed rooftops, and the faint outline of a massive wall stretching along the coastline—Thomas could hardly believe his eyes.

The bustling harbor of Constantinople soon came into full view, a labyrinth of ships, docks, and warehouses filled with goods from across the world. It was a kaleidoscope of colors and sounds—sailors shouting, merchants calling out, the rhythm of hammers striking wood in the distance. As the ship pulled into port, Thomas felt an electric current run through him. This was it. The city he had long imagined was real, standing before him in all its glory.

"Prepare to dock," Giovanni called to the crew. His voice was firm, but there was a spark of excitement in his eyes, too. He had been to Constantinople before, but Thomas could tell that the city still held a special allure for him.

The crew quickly sprang into action, securing the ropes and lowering the gangplank. Giovanni led the way as they disembarked, Thomas close behind. The heat of the midday sun hit him like a wave, and the moment he stepped onto the solid ground of the city, he was surrounded by a sensory overload. The air was thick with the scent of spices—cinnamon, cumin, and saffron—mixing with the earthy tang of the nearby sea. The noise was almost deafening—dozens of languages tangled in the air as traders, locals, and travelers bustled through the streets.

Giovanni turned to Thomas with a knowing smile. "This is Constantinople. A city where the world meets."

Thomas could hardly speak. His mouth was dry as he took in the sight of the Grand Bazaar, its immense archways and narrow alleys leading to hidden courtyards filled with goods from every corner of the known world. The sounds of coins clinking, the clamor of merchants negotiating, and the rhythmic beating of hammers in nearby blacksmith shops blended into a symphony of life.

As they walked deeper into the city, Thomas felt himself caught up in the tide of people. He had spent most of his life in Venice, where the pace was steady, where the canals were familiar, and the smells of saltwater and fish were constant. But here in Constantinople, everything was new—each street, each face, each shop window filled with treasures from distant lands.

Giovanni led them toward a small market square, a stone's throw away from the Grand Bazaar. There, he greeted an old friend—a tall, broad-shouldered man with a thick beard and a wide, welcoming grin. He stood behind a simple stall covered in colorful cloths, piled high with spices, fruits, and silks. The merchant's dark eyes twinkled with recognition as he embraced Giovanni.

"Ah, Giovanni! It's good to see you again, my old friend. And your crew, too, I see. Welcome back to Constantinople!"

"Thank you, Omar," Giovanni replied, his voice warm with familiarity. "It's good to be here again. We've come for supplies and, of course, new goods to trade on our journey."

Thomas watched, fascinated, as Giovanni and Omar began to speak in fluent Arabic, discussing everything from the price of silks to the best routes for navigating the dangerous stretches of the Silk Road. Thomas didn't understand every word, but the fluid exchange of language between the two men felt like a dance—a natural, seamless connection. It was clear that Giovanni, with his years of experience as a sailor and merchant, knew this city as well as he knew the back of his hand.

Thomas, feeling slightly out of place in the bustling crowd, ventured further into the market. His eyes were wide with wonder as he took in the sights around him. Merchants from Egypt, Persia, and India shouted in their native tongues, peddling their wares. He marveled at the vibrant spices piled high in baskets—turmeric, ginger, and cinnamon—and the rich textiles that seemed to glow in the sunlight. There were golden coins, rare jewels, and intricate glasswork. And above it all, the smell of roasting meats and freshly baked bread teased his senses.

He paused before a stall overflowing with dried fruits and nuts. The vendor, an elderly man with a thick white beard, smiled as he offered Thomas a handful of figs. The sweet taste of the fruit was unlike anything he had ever known—rich, dense, and warm from the sun.

"You're not from here, are you?" the vendor asked, his voice heavy with an accent Thomas couldn't place.

Thomas smiled. "No, I'm from Venice. I've come to see your city. It's... unlike anything I've ever imagined."

The old man chuckled, his eyes crinkling at the corners. "That's the way of Constantinople. It's always changing, always new. You'll see many things here—things that will make you question what you know. But it's up to you to decide what you take away from it."

His words stuck with Thomas. The city was a place of endless discovery, yes, but it was also a place that would challenge him to grow, to understand not just the world around him, but himself.

As evening fell, the crew gathered at a small tavern near the docks. The lively chatter of the market outside began to quiet, and the sun dipped below the horizon, casting a purple hue over the city. Giovanni raised his cup of wine.

"To new journeys," he said, his voice steady and sure.

"To new journeys," Thomas echoed, the weight of his own adventure settling into his bones.

As the tavern grew quiet and the crew shared stories of their travels, Thomas couldn't help but think of the road ahead. Constantinople had been a dream, a place he had long imagined but never truly understood until now. And yet, he knew there was still so much more to see, so much more to learn. His journey had only just begun, and already, the world was proving to be even grander, and more complex, than he had ever imagined.

Chapter 8: The Sights of the East

The following morning, the sun rose over Constantinople, casting its warm glow across the city's sprawling rooftops. The streets were already bustling, as merchants unloaded their goods, hawking their wares with enthusiasm and the clamor of a new day. The *La Nuova Stella* was docked for the time being, but Thomas could feel the tug of the adventure calling him again, urging him to go further east, just as Marco Polo had done all those years ago.

Giovanni had arranged for a local guide to take them through the streets of the city, to give them a deeper understanding of the cultures that called this place home. The guide was a man named Malik, a tall figure with sharp eyes and an air of quiet confidence. He wore a long robe in shades of deep green and brown, his turban neatly wrapped, and his voice was calm but authoritative as he led the group through the winding streets.

As Thomas followed closely behind, he noticed the subtle differences between this city and Venice. The buildings here were grand but weathered, the walls draped in ivy and rich tapestries. They passed an ancient mosque with intricate tile work that shimmered even in the early morning light. The sound of the muezzin's call to prayer rang through the air, echoing across the narrow streets. It was a sound Thomas had never heard before, but it felt strangely comforting, as if the city itself was alive, speaking to him through its people and their customs.

"This city," Malik said as they walked, "is not just a crossroads of trade, but a meeting place of beliefs, cultures, and histories. Here, you will find the legacy of Alexander the Great, the rise of the Byzantine Empire, and the ancient knowledge of the Greeks and Romans. Every stone you walk upon carries a story."

Thomas was mesmerized by the words. The city felt alive with history, its streets and buildings steeped in tales of empires long past, yet bustling with the energy of the present.

After a few hours of walking, Malik led them to a large, open marketplace. The atmosphere was electric—sellers and traders from all corners of the world crowded around stalls that stretched as far as the eye could see. There were Arabs with silk scarves, Persians selling rare spices, and Indians offering beautifully woven fabrics. The mingling of so many different people, all offering their goods, gave Thomas a glimpse into the vast web of connections that stretched across continents.

"The marketplace is where everything converges," Malik explained. "What you see here today was once transported over mountains, through deserts, and across seas. This is the heart of the Silk Road."

Thomas felt as though he had stepped into another world, where the East and West weren't just connected by land but by a network of ideas, goods, and cultures. The air was rich with the smells of incense and roasted meat, mingling with the earthy scent of leather and wood. The merchants shouted in a dozen different languages, bargaining with eager customers, while Thomas's senses were overwhelmed by the kaleidoscope of colors that surrounded him.

Giovanni motioned to Thomas, "Stay close. The market can be overwhelming, but it's a good opportunity to see how the world interacts. You'll notice that these traders, though from different places, understand one another through the language of trade."

Thomas nodded, though his eyes were wide as he observed the diverse people around him. An elderly woman in a long, flowing dress offered him a wooden figurine of a horse, its intricately carved surface gleaming in the sunlight. Another merchant gestured to a woven rug, its pattern a swirl of blues and reds that reminded Thomas of the ocean back home.

"You see," Giovanni continued, "this is the Silk Road in its true form. Not just a physical road, but a way of life—a bridge between cultures, ideas, and goods."

As they made their way through the market, Thomas found himself drawn to a small stall in the corner, where a man was selling rare herbs and spices. The merchant, a middle-aged man with a well-groomed beard, spoke to Giovanni in a language Thomas couldn't understand. The air around them was thick with the scent of cumin, cardamom, and coriander.

"This is my friend Hakim," Giovanni said, introducing the merchant with a smile. "He comes from Persia and sells the finest spices in Constantinople."

Hakim nodded and smiled warmly at Thomas. "You are a traveler, yes?" he asked in heavily accented Venetian. "I can see it in your eyes. The desire to see the world."

Thomas chuckled, surprised by how well Hakim spoke his language. "Yes," he said, "I've traveled from Venice, and now I find myself here, in Constantinople."

Hakim's eyes twinkled. "Ah, Venice," he said thoughtfully, "a city of canals and merchants. But here, you will see that the world is much larger than Venice. The Silk Road stretches from the shores of China to the markets of Egypt. And here, in this very market, you will find treasures from every corner of it."

He handed Thomas a small vial of rosewater, its delicate fragrance filling the air. "This is from the gardens of Shiraz," Hakim said. "A gift, to remind you of the beauty of the world you seek to understand."

Thomas took the vial, holding it carefully in his hands. The gesture was small, but it carried a weight that made him pause. In that moment, he realized that he wasn't just collecting treasures for his journey; he was collecting experiences, friendships, and memories that would shape him forever.

As the day wore on, Giovanni and Malik led the group to a large caravanserai—a kind of rest stop for travelers and traders along the Silk Road. Inside, Thomas marveled at the grand architecture. The vaulted ceilings, the intricately decorated tilework, and the large open courtyard filled with merchants from all over. It was a place of rest for those who traveled great distances, a meeting point for the endless flow of goods and stories.

"We'll rest here for the night," Giovanni said, as they found a spot in the courtyard. "Tomorrow, we continue our journey through the lands of the Mongols."

Thomas sat down, feeling the weight of the day settle in. Constantinople had opened his eyes to the vastness of the world, to the endless paths of trade, knowledge, and culture that stretched far beyond the horizons he had once known. But there was still so much more to see. Beyond the city lay the deserts, the mountains, and the lands of the Mongols, where the road would stretch even farther.

As the sun began to set, casting long shadows across the courtyard, Thomas felt a sense of peace wash over him. The journey was far from over, and the road ahead would be filled with challenges and discoveries. But for the first time since he had left Venice, he felt truly ready to embrace the unknown.

Chapter 9: The Desert Crossing

The next morning, the *La Nuova Stella* set sail once again, leaving behind the misty shores of Constantinople. The cool winds that had greeted them in the harbor began to shift as the ship sailed further south and east. Soon, the sea became calmer, and the horizon seemed to stretch endlessly ahead of them. The crew went about their duties, but Thomas felt an undeniable shift in the air—the great adventure that lay ahead now felt different. The seas would soon give way to vast, arid lands. His voyage was about to take a new turn, one that would test his resolve more than any of the seas they had already crossed.

They arrived in the port city of Tabriz, nestled at the northern edge of the Persian Desert. Thomas had heard of the famed Persian Desert, its barren dunes and scorching heat. He'd seen maps of it, but now it felt real—this was a place where life itself seemed to shrink away, leaving only the wind and the sand. He could already feel the dryness in the air and a sense of awe mixed with anxiety in his chest.

"This is where we must part ways with the sea," Giovanni said, his voice tinged with the same unease that Thomas felt. "From here, we'll continue overland, into the heart of Persia. But we'll be in the hands of the desert for many days."

Thomas listened attentively, trying to wrap his mind around the unfamiliar path. They had secured camels for the journey—a sturdy and reliable form of transportation through such a harsh landscape. The caravan consisted of not just Giovanni and his crew, but also a small group of Persian traders and a few merchants who had been making their own way east. They all gathered around a campfire the first night in Tabriz, preparing for the long journey ahead.

The desert felt like a world in itself, separate from everything Thomas had known. He had read about it in books, heard stories about it from the traders, but nothing could compare to standing on its edge, looking out at the undulating dunes that seemed to stretch into infinity.

They set off the next morning, the heat beginning to rise as the sun climbed higher into the sky. The rhythm of the journey was unlike anything Thomas had experienced before. The soft, slow movement of the camels beneath him was both calming and unnerving. The air was thick with dust, and the constant gusts of wind seemed to carry whispers from the past, stories of those who had crossed these desert plains long before him.

The first few days passed in a haze of blistering heat and windblown dust. The caravan stopped at oases when they could, their waters and shaded groves offering a brief respite. Thomas marveled at how the desert could be so unforgiving, yet so full of life at the same time. At each oasis, there were always people—traders, wanderers, and travelers like him—each with their own story and purpose.

As the days wore on, the heat became more oppressive. The ground shimmered in the distance, and the sky above seemed to stretch wider than any sky he had ever seen. The air was dry, thick with the scent of sand and earth, and every step they took seemed to bring them deeper into a place that had no end. The caravan moved in silence, the sound of camels' hooves the only noise breaking the stillness.

One evening, as the sun began to set and the temperature dropped, Giovanni called for a stop. They set up camp in a small valley between the dunes, and a few of the traders set about making a simple meal over the fire. The rest of the group gathered around, settling in for the night.

Thomas, however, found it hard to rest. The vast desert stretched out around him, and something about the sheer emptiness of it unsettled him. He stood at the edge of their camp, watching the shifting dunes in the distance, feeling the cold desert air on his face. He could almost hear the silence pressing in on him, as though the desert itself were speaking, though in a language he couldn't understand.

Giovanni joined him, his dark eyes scanning the horizon. "It's a hard place to understand, isn't it?"

Thomas nodded. "It's so... empty. It feels like it goes on forever."

"It does," Giovanni said quietly. "The desert can be both cruel and beautiful. It will challenge you, but it will also teach you things. You'll learn what it means to survive, to adapt. There's more to this place than just sand and heat. If you look closely, you'll find it."

Thomas turned to him. "What do you mean?"

Giovanni smiled softly, as if recalling something from his own youth. "The desert is a place of endurance. It strips you of everything except what's necessary to survive. When you've crossed it, you understand the world differently. It's as if the earth speaks to you through the challenges it sets before you."

The words stuck with Thomas, and for the rest of the evening, he sat by the fire, contemplating the meaning of Giovanni's words. He had always thought of adventure as something that came with tangible rewards—sights to see, things to find. But now, standing in the midst of the desert, he understood that the greatest rewards of travel came not from external treasures, but from within. The desert would force him to confront his own limits, to dig deep inside himself and discover what he was truly capable of.

The following days grew even more grueling. The caravan passed through stretches of land that seemed to have no life at all. The heat became unbearable, the air a furnace that sucked away what little moisture remained in their bodies. By midday, the camels trudged slowly, their shadows long against the sand. They would rest in the shade of the few sparse trees or rocks they could find, drinking water in short sips to preserve what little they had.

On the fourth day, disaster struck. A sandstorm hit without warning, the winds howling like a living thing. The sand stung against their skin, blurring their vision and choking the air. The caravan was forced to find shelter as quickly as possible, but it was clear that they had lost their bearings. The storm raged for hours, leaving them stranded in the shifting dunes.

When the storm finally passed, the desert had swallowed the traces of their path. They were lost.

Chapter 10: The Mongol Empire

The day after the sandstorm, Thomas woke to a world that was both terrifying and awe-inspiring. The vastness of the desert was now palpable; it seemed to stretch on forever in every direction, a great ocean of sand. The caravan had managed to find shelter, huddling together beneath the sparse cover of a rock outcrop, but their situation had grown desperate. The storm had obliterated all signs of their previous path.

Giovanni, ever the experienced guide, seemed unnerved but determined. He spoke in low tones with the other merchants, exchanging words in a language that Thomas didn't fully understand. The desert had humbled them all, but it hadn't broken them yet.

"We have no choice but to head north," Giovanni finally announced, his voice steady but betraying a hint of uncertainty. "There are nomadic tribes up there, and they might help us. If we're lucky, we'll find water soon enough."

The group packed up what little they had left—water, food, and the few supplies that remained—and set off again. Each day felt like a battle against the elements, each step heavier than the last. The sun beat down mercilessly, and the wind swept the sand into the air, creating mirages that distorted their sense of direction.

For several days, they trudged through the unyielding desert, the pace slow and exhausting. There was little conversation among the travelers. Everyone seemed lost in their thoughts, weighed down by the relentless heat and the oppressive silence that hung in the air. Thomas kept his head low, focused on the camel beneath him, counting the steps of the animal as it plodded along the endless dunes.

Just as he thought he couldn't go on any longer, the desert seemed to shift in a way he hadn't anticipated. A great dark line appeared on the horizon, breaking the monotony of sand. At first, he thought it was a mirage—a trick of the sun—but as they drew closer, the shape of distant mountains became clearer. And beyond them, something even more remarkable.

“It’s the Mongol Empire,” Giovanni muttered to himself, almost as if in awe.

Thomas’s eyes widened. He had heard of the Mongols, but he had never imagined he would be so close to their lands. The Mongols were a nomadic people who had swept across much of Asia, uniting vast territories under their rule. Their empire was the largest in the world, stretching across deserts and steppes, all the way to China. He had heard whispers of their ferocity, their incredible warriors, and their far-reaching influence, but seeing it before him—feeling it in the air—was something entirely different.

Giovanni seemed nervous. "These are not just any lands. These are the lands of Kublai Khan himself. The Mongol Empire is both vast and volatile. We must be careful, and we must be respectful."

The closer they got to the mountains, the more Thomas could feel the weight of the empire’s presence. It wasn’t just a place—it was an idea, an unstoppable force that seemed to stretch out in all directions. As they passed through the barren terrain, they encountered Mongol scouts, their horses swift and their eyes sharp. Giovanni exchanged greetings with them in their language, and they were allowed to continue, albeit with the understanding that they were under the watchful eye of the Mongol Empire.

When they finally reached the Mongol camp, Thomas’s heart raced in excitement and trepidation. The camp stretched out for miles, with tents arranged in orderly rows. Horsemen rode past, their faces impassive beneath their fur-lined hats, while women and children went about their tasks, preparing food and tending to animals. The air was thick with the scent of smoke and cooking, and the sound of voices speaking in harsh, unfamiliar tones echoed around them.

Giovanni led the group through the camp, his posture respectful. They were escorted to a large tent where a Mongol chieftain sat, his face hidden beneath a veil of fur. He looked at them with sharp, calculating eyes.

"You are travelers from afar," the chieftain said, his voice deep and measured. "What brings you to the lands of the Mongols?"

Giovanni bowed deeply. "We seek water and shelter, my lord. The desert has tested us, but we are not without hope. We have heard of your kindness to those who come in peace."

The chieftain studied them for a long moment, and Thomas felt a chill run through him. This was not a man who gave mercy easily.

At last, the chieftain spoke again. "You are lucky to have made it this far. The desert does not forgive. You may stay for a time, but be warned: the Mongol Empire is not a place for weakness. If you do not prove yourselves, you will leave empty-handed."

The words struck Thomas like a blow. He had always thought of himself as brave, but standing before the Mongol chieftain, he felt like a child. The desert had tested him, but this—this was something else entirely.

"Thank you, my lord," Giovanni said, bowing again. "We will do whatever is necessary to prove ourselves worthy."

Over the next few days, Thomas learned more about the Mongols and their incredible empire. He marveled at their skill in horse riding, watching in awe as they rode effortlessly across the plains, their horses swift and strong. The Mongols were a people of the land—practical, resourceful, and incredibly disciplined. They lived off the land, using their herds of cattle and horses for sustenance, and they understood the harshness of the environment better than anyone.

Giovanni and the other traders were busy negotiating with the Mongols, exchanging goods and stories of their travels. Thomas had the chance to speak with some of the young Mongol men, and they told him tales of their warriors, their military conquests, and the great leaders who had shaped their empire. Thomas was fascinated by the vastness of the Mongol Empire and the strength of its people. He had never imagined that the world could be so different from Venice—and yet, here it was, in full view.

One afternoon, Giovanni took Thomas aside. "You must understand, Thomas, that the Mongols are not simply conquerors. They are survivors, and their strength lies in their unity. The world outside the Mongol Empire is fractured—full of kingdoms and cities fighting for power. But the Mongols have learned to stand together, to become something greater than themselves. There is much we can learn from them."

Thomas nodded, absorbing the lesson. It was becoming clear that his journey was not just about the places he would see—it was about the lessons he would learn along the way.

As the caravan prepared to leave the Mongol camp, Thomas looked back one last time. The Empire of the Mongols seemed to stretch into the distance, an endless sea of possibility and power. He had only glimpsed a small part of it, but already, he could feel its presence lingering in the air, its lessons etched into his mind. There was so much more to the world than Venice, and he was only beginning to understand it.

Chapter 11: The City of Kublai Khan

The Mongol Empire's vastness was difficult to comprehend until Thomas stood at its heart—the legendary court of Kublai Khan. After days of traversing the endless steppes, crossing barren plains, and navigating difficult mountain passes, the caravan finally arrived at the imperial city of Shangdu. The city, perched near the northern edge of China, seemed like a dream—a breathtaking symbol of the Mongol Empire's might and opulence.

Thomas had heard many stories about Kublai Khan—how he had expanded the empire and founded the Yuan Dynasty in China, how he was said to be both a great conqueror and a fair ruler. But standing on the outskirts of Shangdu, Thomas realized that the grandeur of the place could not be captured in any story or legend. The city stretched out before him, its high walls rising from the earth like a mountain of stone. Tall towers stood like sentinels, watching over the bustling streets below.

Giovanni, who had been to Kublai Khan's court before, motioned for the caravan to halt. "We must show respect," he warned, his voice low. "This is the heart of the Mongol Empire. Treat it with reverence, and remember that the Khan's word is law."

They were met by Mongol soldiers at the gates, dressed in heavy armor and carrying weapons that gleamed in the sunlight. Their presence alone was enough to send a shiver through Thomas, but Giovanni's calm demeanor seemed to put everyone at ease. They passed through the gates and into the heart of Shangdu.

The city was a marvelous contradiction. While the streets were filled with vendors selling goods from across the empire—exotic silks, fragrant spices, precious gems—the air also carried the scent of horses, of sweat, of hard work. It was a place of great wealth and sophistication, yet there was an underlying sense of raw power and survival that permeated everything.

They made their way toward the imperial palace, a massive complex of ornate buildings with gold-tipped roofs and walls covered in intricate murals depicting scenes of Mongol warriors riding into battle. The walls were lined with banners of the Khan's emblem: a golden sun encircled by a dragon.

As they entered the palace grounds, Thomas's senses were overwhelmed. The size of the place, the bustling servants, the opulent decorations—it was like stepping into another world. The air was filled with the sounds of people speaking in rapid Mongolian, and the scent of incense and cooking wafted from nearby kitchens. There were musicians playing strange instruments, and the laughter of courtiers could be heard from the courtyard.

The group was led through a grand hall into an inner chamber, where Kublai Khan himself sat upon an elevated throne, surrounded by his advisors. He was not what Thomas had expected. The stories had described him as a fearsome conqueror, a man of war and strategy, yet before Thomas sat a ruler of quiet dignity. His face was solemn, yet his eyes sparkled with intelligence. He was dressed in rich silks, his robe embroidered with golden dragons, and a crown made of precious stones rested atop his head.

Giovanni, ever the diplomat, bowed deeply to the Khan, and Thomas followed his example, his heart pounding in his chest. This was a moment he had never anticipated—standing before the most powerful man in the world.

"You have come from afar," Kublai Khan said in a voice that was calm but carried the weight of authority. "What brings you to my court?"

Giovanni spoke, recounting their journey and their desire to trade goods, seeking the Khan's approval to continue their journey. But Thomas, too overwhelmed to speak, simply stood in awe. He could hardly believe he was in the presence of Kublai Khan, whose decisions shaped the course of nations.

After a long pause, the Khan turned his gaze to Thomas. "And you, boy—what is your name?"

"Thomas, my lord," Thomas managed to say, his voice sounding small in the great hall.

The Khan nodded, his eyes gleaming with curiosity. "Thomas, you have crossed the vastness of my empire and stood in my presence. What is it that you seek?"

Thomas hesitated. There was so much he wanted to say—so many questions, so much wonder inside him. He had journeyed so far and seen so much already, but this moment felt different. The Mongols were more than conquerors. They were survivors, explorers, and warriors who had unified much of the known world. He wanted to ask the Khan about his empire, about the great journeys of his ancestors, and about the world that lay beyond.

"I seek to understand, my lord," Thomas finally said, his voice quiet but earnest. "I wish to learn the ways of your people, to understand how such an empire can rise from the ground."

The Khan's eyes twinkled with amusement, and he leaned forward slightly, as if intrigued by the young boy's honesty. "You are wise for one so young. The empire is built not on strength alone but on the unity of its people. The Mongols are a people of great diversity—united by a single purpose, to live freely and with honor."

He paused, as if contemplating something for a moment. Then he gestured to one of his advisors, who stepped forward and handed him a scroll.

"Thomas Polo," the Khan said, his voice carrying the weight of destiny. "Your journey has brought you to me. Perhaps it is fate that you have come. You are welcome in my court, and I will see that you are given a guide who will show you the inner workings of my empire. You may stay and learn, but remember: knowledge is power. Use it wisely."

Thomas's heart raced with excitement. He had come to the Mongol Empire seeking adventure, seeking answers. Now, Kublai Khan himself had opened the door for him to learn and grow in ways he had never imagined. This was no longer just a journey to see the world—it was a chance to understand the forces that shaped it.

The next few weeks in Shangdu were filled with learning and discovery. Thomas spent his days in the presence of scholars, military commanders, and traders. He learned of the Mongols' impressive system of communication, their extensive network of horse riders who could send messages across the empire in mere days. He marveled at the way the Khan had structured his empire, with different cultures and people living under a common law.

He also had the opportunity to meet other travelers—merchants, diplomats, and even explorers from distant lands who had made the arduous journey to Kublai Khan's court. These men and women, like Thomas, were in search of knowledge, and they shared their stories of faraway lands—India, Persia, the steppes of Mongolia, and beyond.

It was during one of these evenings, as the sun dipped below the horizon, that Giovanni approached Thomas with an important message.

"Thomas," Giovanni said, his voice low and serious. "The Khan has made arrangements for us. We will travel further into the empire, to the city of Xanadu, the summer capital. It is a place of great beauty and learning. And I've arranged for you to accompany us."

Thomas could hardly believe his ears. The Khan's summer palace in Xanadu was legendary. It was said to be filled with gardens, libraries, and the most exquisite works of art. It was the next step in his journey—a place where he could learn more about the Mongol way of life and, perhaps, begin to understand the deeper mysteries of the world.

With renewed purpose, Thomas prepared to leave Shangdu. He knew that the journey ahead would challenge him in ways he could not yet comprehend. But he was no longer just a boy from Venice. He was a traveler—a seeker of knowledge, a witness to the marvels of the world.

As the caravan prepared to depart, Thomas looked out across the Mongol plains, the vastness of the empire stretching before him. The journey had only just begun.

Chapter 12: The Unfamiliar Paths

As the caravan left the grand city of Shangdu and began its journey toward Xanadu, Thomas could hardly contain his excitement. The journey was long, but every day felt like an opportunity to learn something new, something he had never encountered before. The vast Mongol Empire was like nothing he had ever seen, and every mile brought new faces, new customs, and new landscapes. But it was not just the vastness of the empire that was awe-inspiring; it was the interconnectedness of it all.

The caravan traveled through dense forests, crossing rivers that glistened under the morning sun, and over vast plains that seemed to stretch into eternity. The weather varied dramatically, from freezing cold at night to scorching heat during the day. But despite the hardships, there was an undeniable sense of awe in the air. Thomas could see how the Mongol Empire had been forged—through persistence, strategy, and, most of all, unity.

As they moved deeper into the heart of the empire, they passed through regions that were unfamiliar to Thomas. In the western part of the empire, they encountered the Turkic peoples, with their distinctive clothing, bright turbans, and intricate jewelry. The traders from these regions spoke a language that sounded both harsh and melodic at the same time, and their markets were filled with exotic goods from Persia, Central Asia, and beyond.

One morning, as they crossed a narrow mountain pass, Thomas met an old merchant who told him of a journey that had taken him from the farthest reaches of Europe to the heart of China. The merchant's name was Iskander, and his face was lined with wrinkles, but his eyes still held the gleam of a man who had seen much and learned even more.

"You are a traveler, boy," Iskander said to Thomas as they walked side by side, their horses plodding along the rocky path. "But you do not yet understand the meaning of travel. It is not just about moving from one place to another. It is about moving inside yourself. The world is full of wonders, but it is only through learning, and growing, that we can begin to understand those wonders."

Thomas listened intently, trying to grasp the deeper meaning of the merchant's words. He had thought of travel as a way to escape, to see the world and experience the unknown. But Iskander's words made him realize that travel was more than just an external journey—it was a journey within.

Over the following days, the caravan continued eastward, and Thomas had the chance to learn more about the Mongols' unique way of life. They traveled with great efficiency, their horses swift and tireless, and their guides expert in navigating the harsh terrain. The Mongols seemed to have a deep understanding of the land they lived on—how to read the signs of the weather, how to predict where the best grazing lands would be, how to find water in even the driest of deserts.

Giovanni, who had been teaching Thomas about the customs of the Mongols, took the opportunity to explain more about their military prowess. "The Mongols are not just conquerors," Giovanni said one evening as they sat around the campfire, the stars twinkling above them. "They are brilliant strategists. Their army is built on speed, mobility, and discipline. It is said that Kublai Khan could send a thousand riders in any direction and have them return with intelligence about their enemies in a matter of days."

Thomas listened with fascination as Giovanni spoke of the Mongol horse archers, their ability to strike from a distance and move swiftly across the battlefield. It was a new kind of warfare—different from anything Thomas had seen or heard of before.

But there was something else that caught Thomas's attention. It wasn't just the military might or the vastness of the empire—it was the way the Mongols treated their people. Everywhere they traveled, Thomas saw evidence of a society built on merit and respect for all its members. Whether a person was a trader from Persia, a warrior from the steppes, or a farmer from China, everyone had a place in the empire. Thomas began to understand why the Mongol Empire had been so successful—it wasn't just the strength of its warriors, but the unity of its people.

One evening, as the caravan made camp near the edge of a vast desert, Thomas stood by the fire, gazing out at the endless expanse of sand. The wind had picked up, and the air was thick with the scent of dust. He had never seen anything like this before—an ocean of sand that seemed to stretch out into the horizon without end.

Giovanni walked up beside him, sensing his awe. "This is the Persian Desert, Thomas," Giovanni said quietly. "It is a place of great beauty, but also great danger. Many who attempt to cross it without preparation do not make it."

Thomas nodded, his eyes scanning the horizon. "I can feel the danger. The land seems alive—like it's waiting for something."

Giovanni smiled. "It is alive, in its own way. And it will teach you things you cannot learn in any city or palace. The desert has a way of humbling even the greatest of men."

Over the next few days, the caravan slowly made its way through the desert. Thomas could feel the harshness of the land with every step, as the heat of the sun beat down during the day, and the coldness of the night crept into his bones. But there was something beautiful about it, too. The endless dunes, the silence, the way the stars seemed to shine brighter in the absence of light pollution—it was a different kind of beauty, a beauty that spoke to the soul.

As they traveled deeper into the desert, Thomas began to understand what Giovanni had meant. The desert was not just a physical challenge—it was a mental and spiritual one. It forced him to confront his own fears, his own weaknesses. Every day was a battle against the elements, against exhaustion, and against the fear of the unknown. But it was also a place of profound clarity. In the silence of the desert, Thomas began to reflect on his journey—on all the places he had been, the people he had met, and the lessons he had learned.

In a way, the desert was teaching him something deeper about himself—that the true journey was not just about the places he visited, but about the person he was becoming. He was no longer just a boy from Venice who dreamed of adventure. He was becoming someone who understood the world in a way he never could have imagined before.

But just as the desert seemed to stretch on forever, so did the road ahead. As the caravan continued toward Xanadu, Thomas knew that the journey was far from over. There were more challenges to face, more people to meet, and more lessons to learn.

And so, with the vastness of the Mongol Empire stretching out before him, Thomas Polo set his eyes on the horizon, ready to walk the unfamiliar paths that lay ahead.

Chapter 13: The Great Wall of China

After weeks of travel, the caravan finally reached the northern borders of the Chinese Empire. The vastness of the land, the rugged terrain, and the mystery that lay ahead filled Thomas with a mixture of awe and anticipation. It wasn't just the people they encountered along the way, nor the rolling landscapes—they were now nearing one of the most legendary landmarks in the world, the Great Wall of China.

As they approached the Wall, Thomas felt a sense of reverence. The structure was more magnificent than he could have ever imagined. It stretched across the mountains, winding like a giant serpent through the landscape. The Wall was not merely a fortification; it was a symbol of the might and determination of the Chinese people. It had stood for centuries, a silent guardian against invaders, and now Thomas was standing at its base, gazing up at its towering presence.

Giovanni, who had traveled the Silk Road many times before, seemed unfazed by the Wall's grandeur, but he could see the effect it had on Thomas. "You see, Thomas," he said, "this wall is more than just stone and mortar. It represents the strength of a civilization that, for centuries, has sought to protect its people from the dangers of the outside world. It was built by emperors and warriors, artisans and laborers—all working together to protect their homes and families."

Thomas nodded, feeling the weight of history in the air. He had heard stories about the Wall, but standing in its shadow made those stories feel real. He walked along its length, his hand brushing against the ancient stones, each one worn down by the passage of time. The Wall seemed to whisper stories of battles fought, of sacrifices made, and of an unyielding resolve.

Giovanni led him up a steep incline toward one of the watchtowers. From there, Thomas could see the vast expanse of China spreading out below him. The mountains, the forests, and the fields stretched for miles, and in the distance, he could make out the faint outline of the great city of Dadu, the capital of the Yuan Dynasty.

As they sat on the steps of the tower, Giovanni began to explain more about the importance of the Wall. "This was not the work of a single emperor or a single generation. It took hundreds of years to build, with different dynasties contributing to its construction. The Wall represents the Chinese people's enduring spirit. It's a reminder that great achievements are born from persistence, from the belief that even the most insurmountable challenges can be overcome."

Thomas absorbed every word, feeling as though the very air around him was filled with lessons. The Great Wall was not just a physical barrier—it was a metaphor for the challenges that lay ahead. He realized that his journey was not unlike the building of the Wall. It would require persistence, resilience, and determination. There would be obstacles and hardships, but the wall itself stood as a testament to what could be achieved when a vision was pursued with unwavering commitment.

As the sun began to set, casting a warm golden glow over the land, Giovanni turned to Thomas with a thoughtful expression. "You are young, Thomas, but already you are learning the most important lesson of all—how to face challenges with courage and perseverance. There are many more obstacles ahead, but remember that every journey, no matter how difficult, has its rewards."

Thomas smiled, his heart swelling with a newfound sense of purpose. He had always thought that traveling the world was about seeing exotic places and meeting interesting people. But now, standing at the Great Wall of China, he understood that the true value of the journey was not in the destinations, but in the lessons learned along the way. The world was vast and filled with challenges, but with each challenge, he was growing stronger, wiser, and more capable of navigating the paths that lay before him.

The next morning, the caravan set out again, heading deeper into China. But as they traveled, Thomas could not shake the image of the Great Wall from his mind. It had become a symbol of what he was striving for—an unbreakable resolve to continue moving forward, no matter how difficult the journey might become.

The further they traveled, the more Thomas began to understand the significance of his own journey. He was not just exploring foreign lands; he was exploring the very limits of his own strength and potential. Each new experience, each new culture, each new challenge, was shaping him into the man he was becoming.

But the Great Wall was only one part of the larger puzzle. China, as Giovanni had said, was vast, and there were still many mysteries to uncover, many lessons to learn.

The caravan made its way toward the city of Dadu, and Thomas couldn't help but feel the excitement building within him. He was on the verge of entering a world that was both foreign and familiar, a world that had once seemed like a distant dream, but was now within his reach. The Mongol Empire, with all its complexity and wonder, was opening its doors to him. And as he stood on the brink of this new chapter, he realized that he was no longer just a boy with a dream—he was an explorer, a learner, and a witness to the greatness of the world.

Chapter 14: A Storm on the Horizon

The sun hung low on the horizon as the caravan made its way across the plains of northern China. The air was thick with the scent of wild herbs and distant smoke, as traders and travelers filled the roads, each heading toward their own destination. But as the day drew to a close, the calm was shattered by an ominous change in the weather.

Thomas had always been accustomed to the unpredictability of life on the open sea, but this was different. The air felt heavy, as if the earth itself were holding its breath. Giovanni, who had become a trusted companion in these long months of travel, stopped suddenly, his hand raised in warning.

"Storm's coming," Giovanni muttered, his face grim.

Thomas looked up at the sky, noticing the deepening clouds that seemed to stretch endlessly toward the horizon. The usual calm of the landscape was replaced by a restless energy, the wind picking up as if whispering a warning of the danger that lay ahead.

"Do you think it will be bad?" Thomas asked, his voice tinged with concern.

Giovanni's expression was unreadable, but there was a hardened edge to his words. "When you've been on the road as long as I have, you learn to respect the power of nature. This storm isn't a small one, Thomas. We'll need to find shelter and prepare."

Without wasting any time, the caravan's leader, an experienced Mongol merchant named Jebe, gave orders for the group to gather their belongings and set up a makeshift camp. Thomas helped with the preparations, feeling the tension in the air as the wind began to howl. The once tranquil landscape now felt like an alien world, as though the earth itself had transformed into something hostile and unpredictable.

As the first raindrops fell, cold and sharp, Thomas hurried to shelter under a canvas tarp with Giovanni and the rest of the caravan members. They huddled together, watching the sky darken to an almost unnatural shade of black. The storm was upon them in a matter of minutes, the rain coming in torrents, accompanied by violent gusts of wind that sent sand and debris swirling through the air.

For hours, the storm raged around them, the wind howling like a wild animal and the rain drumming against the tarps with an incessant rhythm. Thomas could feel the fear creeping into his chest, but he forced it down. He had faced danger before, but this was different. This storm felt as though it could tear everything apart.

At one point, a great flash of lightning lit up the sky, followed by a deafening crack of thunder that made the ground tremble beneath their feet. Thomas's heart raced. The force of nature was unlike anything he had ever encountered. It was raw, untamed, and beyond human control.

As the night wore on, Thomas lay awake, staring up at the storm's fury. He couldn't help but think back to the Great Wall and the lessons he had learned there. The Wall was strong, but it had been built to withstand the forces of nature, not the forces of time and change. In that moment, Thomas realized that the same lessons applied to him. No matter how strong he thought he was, he, too, was vulnerable to the world around him. But vulnerability didn't mean weakness—it meant resilience. He had learned that the world was full of dangers, but that didn't mean he should shrink from them. If anything, it meant he needed to rise to meet them, head-on.

As the storm raged on, Thomas's thoughts turned to his father. Antonio Polo had spent his life working with his hands, building ships, and enduring the hardships of the sea. He had never been one to show weakness, and Thomas admired that strength. But now, as he lay in the dark, listening to the storm that seemed to rage without end, Thomas understood something deeper. His father's strength was not just in his ability to build ships or fight through hardships—it was in his ability to persevere, to stand firm in the face of adversity, to never back down.

The storm finally began to subside in the early hours of the morning, leaving behind a world washed clean by the rain. The sky lightened, and the winds died down, leaving an eerie calm in their wake. Giovanni emerged from under the tarp, stretching his stiff limbs.

"We've made it through," he said quietly, looking out at the wet, glistening landscape. "But that storm was a reminder, Thomas. The world will test you in ways you never imagined. And when it does, you need to remember that the storm always passes. But what's left behind is the real test. Are you strong enough to pick up the pieces, to continue on when the world seems broken?"

Thomas nodded, understanding the depth of Giovanni's words. This journey was about more than just the destinations—they were about the trials along the way, the lessons that came with each challenge. The storm had shown him how small and fragile he was in the face of nature, but it had also shown him that he could survive, that he could stand tall even when the world seemed to be crashing down around him.

As the caravan packed up and continued on their journey, Thomas felt a renewed sense of determination. The storm had been a brutal test, but it had also strengthened him. He knew now that the journey ahead would be full of similar storms—both literal and figurative. But he was ready. He was no longer the boy who had boarded the ship in Venice with only dreams of adventure. He was becoming the man who could face whatever the world threw at him.

The storm was over. The path ahead was uncertain, but it was his to walk.

Chapter 15: The Heart of the Silk Road

The journey eastward had been long and arduous, but now, the caravan was approaching a new and exciting chapter: the heart of the legendary Silk Road. The landscape had shifted. Gone were the barren deserts and scorching heat of the Persian plains. Instead, the air grew thicker, the mountains higher, and the roads more trafficked with merchants, travelers, and traders.

For days, Thomas could feel the stir of anticipation in the air as they crossed into the fertile lands of the central Asian steppe. It was a place where the East and West converged, where ideas, goods, and people moved in and out of the ancient cities. He had heard so many stories about this great trading route—the Silk Road, a lifeline that connected distant empires, kingdoms, and cultures. Now, as he moved deeper into this vast network, he understood it was more than just a path for merchants; it was the very thread that wove the world together.

The road was filled with all kinds of travelers—merchants with large carts filled with spices, silk, and fine china, and caravans of traders leading their camels, laden with goods from the distant lands of India and China. There were also wandering pilgrims, soldiers on their way to far-off battles, and scholars seeking knowledge in the great cities of the East. Thomas couldn't help but marvel at the diversity of the people around him—their clothing, their languages, their customs—each one a reminder that the world was far larger and more intricate than he had ever imagined.

One evening, the caravan stopped at an ancient caravanserai, a large inn built specifically to accommodate travelers on this perilous journey. The sun was low in the sky, casting an orange glow over the dusty landscape, as traders unloaded their goods and set up tents for the night. The air was thick with the sounds of haggling, the clinking of metal coins, and the low murmur of languages from across the world.

Thomas had never seen anything like it. The scene was both overwhelming and mesmerizing. He followed Giovanni through the bustling marketplace, where every stall was brimming with exotic goods—brightly colored silks from China, rich fabrics from Persia, spices that made the air fragrant, and intricate pottery from the distant lands of India. As he moved through the marketplace, Thomas was captivated by the stories woven into the fabric of the Silk Road.

"This is where it all happens," Giovanni said, his voice filled with awe as they made their way through the caravanserai. "It's not just about the goods, Thomas. It's about the exchange—ideas, cultures, inventions, and art. Everything you see here has traveled across deserts, mountains, and seas to get here. It's a journey of knowledge as much as it is of trade."

Thomas's eyes scanned the busy streets. He watched a group of merchants from the far east, their faces tanned from the sun, arguing over the price of silk. Nearby, a group of Persian traders huddled over a basket of spices, and a caravan from the Arabian Peninsula unloaded camels laden with fragrant wood. There were also scholars and diplomats from the Mongol Empire, exchanging scrolls and books with traders from Europe.

As they approached a stall, Giovanni paused and pulled Thomas's attention to a set of maps laid out on a wooden table. The merchant, a middle-aged man with a deep voice, looked up and smiled.

"These are the maps of the Silk Road," he said, his accent thick but warm. "I have traveled much of it. From here to Baghdad, from Samarkand to Chang'an. Every road leads to new discoveries."

Thomas leaned over the maps, his fingers tracing the intricate lines that represented ancient trade routes. The vastness of it all seemed impossible to comprehend, but it was also exhilarating. Each line on the map represented a journey—one that had been made by people before him, and one that he would soon follow.

"What do you think, Thomas?" Giovanni asked, noticing his fascination. "What do you see when you look at these maps?"

Thomas hesitated for a moment, taking in the complexity of the roads, the sprawling cities, and the countless connections that spanned continents. He had always thought of the world in terms of places—Venice, the Mediterranean, the East—but now, it seemed as if all of those places were part of a much larger, intricate whole.

"I see... possibility," Thomas finally said. "It's like every road here is a bridge between two worlds. I never realized how connected everything is."

Giovanni smiled, his eyes sparkling with understanding. "That's right. And it's not just about the goods we trade—it's about the bridges we build between different ways of life. The Silk Road isn't just one road. It's a whole series of paths—some traveled by merchants, others by scholars, and others by explorers like you."

As the night fell, the caravanserai began to quiet down. The traders retired to their tents, the clamor of the marketplace dying away as the moon rose over the desert. Thomas sat by the fire, his thoughts swirling around everything he had seen and heard. The Silk Road was more than just a trade route—it was a meeting place for civilizations, where cultures and ideas came together in ways he could never have imagined before.

Giovanni's words echoed in his mind. It wasn't just about traveling from one place to another; it was about what you brought with you, what you learned, and how you connected with the people and the world around you. He had started his journey in search of adventure, following in the footsteps of Marco Polo. But now, he was beginning to understand that the journey was about something far greater than himself—it was about understanding the world in all its complexity and sharing those experiences with others.

The next morning, as the caravan prepared to set out again, Thomas felt a renewed sense of purpose. The road ahead was still long, but with each step, he felt himself growing stronger, more capable of understanding the intricate web of humanity that stretched across the world. The Silk Road was not just a physical journey—it was a journey of the mind, heart, and soul. And Thomas was only just beginning to understand its true power.

As the caravan continued on its way, Thomas looked up at the sky and smiled. The world, vast and interconnected, awaited him—and he was ready.

Chapter 16: The Return Journey

After months of travel, vast stretches of desert, and countless adventures through unfamiliar lands, Thomas felt the pull of home. The exhilarating excitement that had once filled his heart had been replaced with a sense of longing—a quiet yearning for the familiar sights of Venice, for the comfort of his parents' home, and for the life he had left behind. But, he knew that he had changed in ways that he could never have imagined when he first left.

The journey that had begun with such bold enthusiasm now felt different. It was no longer just about following in the footsteps of Marco Polo or chasing the dream of seeing the world. It was about something deeper—about understanding who he was, about seeing the world not just as an explorer but as someone who had lived it. As he began to turn back, he realized that the world he had encountered was not a distant land—it was a part of him now, etched into his soul.

Giovanni, who had been by his side through every twist and turn of the journey, noticed the change in Thomas. There was a quiet sadness in his eyes, a realization that the time to return home had arrived.

"You've changed, Thomas," Giovanni said one evening as they sat by the campfire, the dark sky above them filled with a thousand stars. "The boy who first left Venice is not the same as the one sitting here now."

Thomas smiled, but the smile was bittersweet. "I've seen so much... and I feel like I know so little. It's hard to put into words."

Giovanni nodded. "The journey isn't just about what you see. It's about how you see it—and what you take with you. When I first set out on the road, I thought I would find the answers to all my questions. But as you keep traveling, you learn that there are no simple answers. There's only more to discover."

Thomas stared into the fire, the flames dancing in the still night air. The road ahead, though familiar in the sense that it led toward Venice, no longer felt like the same path he had once eagerly followed. He had learned so much along the way—about the world, its people, and himself—that he could never again see his homeland with the same eyes.

The caravan continued its journey westward, leaving behind the rich cultures of the East. They crossed the vast steppes of Mongolia, the rugged mountains of Central Asia, and the bustling cities of Persia, each step taking them closer to the Mediterranean and to Venice. Along the way, they stopped in familiar cities, but everything felt different now. The trade routes, once unfamiliar and exotic, now felt like chapters in a book he had already read.

As they crossed into the Mediterranean world, Thomas couldn't help but reflect on everything he had learned. The cities of Venice and the West were still there, but they no longer felt as vast and mysterious as they once had. They were a part of a larger world, a world that Thomas now understood was interconnected in ways that could not be seen with the eye alone.

One afternoon, as they neared the Italian coast, Giovanni turned to him once more. "Are you ready to return, Thomas?"

Thomas thought for a moment. The journey had been long, filled with hardships and triumphs, but it had given him more than he could have ever imagined. He had learned that travel was not just about seeing new places—it was about finding the new within yourself, understanding the connections between the distant lands, and discovering the threads that wove humanity together. But there was still more to be learned.

"I am ready," Thomas said, his voice firm yet reflective. "But I know I will never stop exploring. Not really."

Giovanni smiled, a knowing look in his eyes. "No one ever truly stops exploring, my young friend. But sometimes, the greatest journey is the one that takes you back to where you began."

The shores of Italy gradually came into view, the pale blue of the Mediterranean shimmering in the distance. Venice was still far off, but Thomas felt his heart quicken as they sailed toward the place he had left behind. The city was as he remembered—its narrow canals, the bustling marketplace, and the majestic architecture that stood as a testament to its power and glory. But Thomas was no longer the boy who had once dreamed of adventure from the docks. He had traveled the world, seen the grandeur of China, the vastness of the Mongol Empire, and the richness of the cultures that lay in between.

He had lived what few had dared to dream.

As they docked in Venice, a wave of emotions washed over him. There, standing by the docks, was his mother, Lucia, waiting for him. Her face was a mixture of relief and joy, but there was also something more in her eyes—pride. Antonio Polo, his father, stood beside her, a stern yet pleased look on his face.

Thomas stepped off the ship, his legs wobbly from the long voyage. His father's eyes met his, and for the first time, there was no conflict, no tension—only a silent understanding. Antonio clapped him on the shoulder, a rare gesture of warmth.

"You've done it, boy," Antonio said, his voice thick with emotion. "I never thought you'd make it. But I see now... you've become a man, a man of the world."

Thomas smiled, the weight of the journey heavy in his heart, but the future felt brighter than ever. He had returned not only as a son but as a traveler, a storyteller, and an explorer of the world.

"Father, I've learned so much. And I've seen things I never imagined," Thomas said, his voice steady. "But there's still more to be done."

Antonio raised an eyebrow. "More?"

Thomas nodded. "I'm going to write it all down. I want people to know about the world beyond Venice. I want them to see what I've seen, to learn what I've learned."

His father looked at him for a moment, then smiled, shaking his head as if in disbelief. "I guess the journey never really ends."

Thomas looked out over the city of Venice, a place he now understood in ways he never had before. It was a part of the world, connected to every other place by the threads of trade, culture, and human experience. The city had always felt like the center of the universe to him, but now he knew it was just one piece of the grand, interconnected tapestry of the world.

Chapter 17: Lessons from the Journey

As the days turned into weeks, Thomas found himself back in the familiar streets of Venice, but it was a Venice that now seemed to stand still, compared to the vast and ever-changing world he had just explored. It was as if he were seeing his home through new eyes. The sound of the gondoliers' oars gently slicing through the canals, the clamor of merchants haggling over wares, and the smell of fresh bread wafting through the streets—it all felt different. These sights, sounds, and smells, once the daily routine of his life, now seemed like fragments of a world he had left behind, a world he no longer fully belonged to.

It was early one morning when Thomas found himself on the edge of the Grand Canal, watching the boats pass by as the sun slowly rose behind the spires of the city. His thoughts wandered back to his journey, to the people he had met, the places he had seen, and the lessons that had shaped him into the young man he was now.

The world he had encountered on his travels was vast, diverse, and full of wonders beyond imagination. But with every new experience, he had come to realize that the greatest lesson of all had been understanding that the journey was never really about the destinations or the riches one could collect—it was about the connections made, the people met, and the growth that came with each challenge faced.

It was on that morning by the canal that he was joined by Giovanni, who had become more of a brother than a mere fellow traveler over the years.

"Thinking about the road again, are we?" Giovanni asked, his voice as calm and steady as it always was.

Thomas turned to look at him, a smile tugging at the corner of his lips. "I can't help it. It feels strange to be back."

Giovanni nodded in understanding, his eyes thoughtful. "I know what you mean. When you leave a place for so long, it's as if it ceases to be the same place you left. You've changed, and so has it. But there's something about returning home that helps you see it for what it really is."

Thomas glanced out over the water. The city was waking up, and the gondolas glided like slow-moving shadows across the shimmering surface of the canal. "You're right. I've seen so much out there, Giovanni. The people, the places... the worlds within worlds. I thought I would come back with all the answers. But now I know—I'll never have all the answers. There's so much more to learn."

Giovanni smiled softly, the weight of their shared experiences reflected in his eyes. "That's the beauty of it, Thomas. The more you travel, the more you realize that life itself is an endless journey. And the most important thing isn't the destination—it's the wisdom you gather along the way."

The words seemed to sink deep into Thomas's heart. The wisdom, the lessons of the road, were far more valuable than any treasure. It was in the stories told by the old merchants in the bazaars of Samarkand, the warmth of a Mongol warrior's handshake, the wisdom shared by an elderly Chinese traveler by the side of a mountain path—these were the treasures that had truly enriched him.

"I've learned so much," Thomas said slowly. "About the people and cultures I encountered... about the strength of the human spirit. I've seen kindness where I least expected it, and cruelty where I thought there was none. I've learned that the world is vast and full of wonders, but it's also fragile. We're all so connected, Giovanni."

Giovanni nodded in agreement. "The world is bigger than any one person, but it's also smaller than we think. Every person we meet, every place we visit, leaves a mark on us. And we, in turn, leave a mark on them."

Thomas's mind wandered back to the people who had helped him on his journey—old men who shared their wisdom, young traders who offered him food and shelter without a second thought, and the warriors who had protected him when danger was near. All of these people, from every corner of the world, had shown him that the true essence of humanity lay in compassion, understanding, and the willingness to share what little one had with others.

"I want to share what I've learned," Thomas said, a new determination building in his chest. "I've seen so many beautiful things—things that people in Venice would never believe unless they saw it for themselves. I have to tell them. I want to write it all down. Share these stories. These lessons."

Giovanni looked at him with a proud smile. "You have a gift for words, Thomas. Your story will inspire many."

Over the next several weeks, Thomas poured his heart and soul into the pages of a book. He wrote about the people he had met—the merchants and scholars, the emperors and traders, the nomads and warriors. He wrote about the landscapes—the deserts of Persia, the mountains of Central Asia, the palaces of China, and the vast steppes of Mongolia. But most of all, he wrote about the lessons he had learned—the importance of understanding different cultures, the strength of kindness in the face of adversity, and the idea that the world, though vast and diverse, was ultimately a shared space, where every person had a story and every place had a meaning.

As he wrote, Thomas also reflected on the journey itself—the emotions he had felt as he sailed away from Venice, the loneliness and fear that had gnawed at him during the hardest parts of the journey, and the overwhelming sense of awe he had felt upon reaching the court of Kublai Khan. It had been a journey of self-discovery as much as it had been a journey of discovery of the world around him.

And as he wrote the final lines of the book, he understood that the lessons were not just for Venice. They were for anyone willing to listen—to anyone brave enough to explore not just the world, but the heart of what it means to be human.

Chapter 18: The Long-Awaited Return

The streets of Venice were alive with their usual hustle and bustle, but for Thomas, they felt distant, like the faded echoes of a life he had once known. As he walked along the Grand Canal, his mind swirled with the memories of the many lands he had visited and the people he had encountered. He had been to places that most could only dream of, and in return, those places had changed him in ways he never could have imagined.

Returning home was both a relief and a challenge. The familiar sights, sounds, and scents of Venice were comforting, yet they seemed to amplify the distance between him and the young boy who had once sailed away with nothing but dreams in his eyes. He had left as a child, and now, after so many years, he was returning as a man—one who had seen the world in its full glory and its darkest depths.

The Polo family house, nestled in one of the quieter districts of the city, was just as he remembered it. The ivy that clung to the stone walls, the small garden where his mother had once tended to roses, the worn wooden door—everything seemed unchanged. Yet, as he approached it, Thomas felt an uneasy knot in his chest. The journey had been long, and the man who stood at the threshold of his family home was no longer the boy who had left with a heart full of dreams.

His mother, Lucia Polo, was the first to greet him. She stood in the doorway, her face a mixture of joy and relief, her arms outstretched to embrace him. But as she pulled him into a warm hug, Thomas couldn't shake the sense that something was missing.

"You've come back to us, Thomas," she said softly, pulling back to look at him. Her eyes were full of pride, but there was a trace of sadness in them as well.

"I've come back, Mother," Thomas said, his voice thick with emotion. "But I am not the same person who left."

Lucia smiled, her eyes glistening. "I know. I've seen it in your letters. I've seen it in the way you speak of the places you've visited, the people you've met. You've become someone extraordinary."

But as the words left her lips, Thomas could feel the weight of his return bearing down on him. He wasn't sure if he had become extraordinary or if he had simply become someone who could never fully fit back into the life he had once known. The world was so vast, and his journey had taken him to places that no one in Venice could understand.

As he entered the house, he was greeted by the smell of his mother's cooking—simmering herbs, roasted meats, and freshly baked bread. It was a scent he had longed for during his travels, yet now, it filled him with a bittersweet ache.

"Father's waiting for you in the study," Lucia said, her voice gentle. "He's been working on something all morning. I think he's eager to see you too."

Thomas nodded and made his way to the study. Antonio Polo, his father, sat at a large oak desk covered in maps, ship plans, and scrolls. His graying hair and deeply furrowed brow gave him an air of authority, but there was a softness in his eyes as Thomas entered the room.

The two men stood in silence for a moment, looking at each other. For a moment, the years melted away, and Thomas felt the familiar sense of both love and tension that had always existed between them. His father's stern presence had shaped much of his early life, and yet, his father had always been a man of quiet strength and wisdom.

Antonio didn't speak at first, but when he did, his voice was steady. "You've returned, my son. I see you've grown in ways I never imagined."

Thomas smiled faintly, feeling the weight of his father's words. "I have grown, Father. But in ways I didn't expect. I've learned things I never dreamed possible. I've seen the world, and now I understand what it truly means to be part of it."

Antonio nodded slowly, his eyes shifting to the maps on the desk. "I always knew you had the spirit of an explorer in you. When you were a boy, you'd spend hours staring at those maps, dreaming of lands far away. But I didn't know it would take you as far as you've gone."

Thomas's heart swelled with a mixture of pride and sadness. "I followed the path I believed in, Father. But I've come to realize that the world is much more complicated than I ever imagined. There's so much more to discover—about people, cultures, and ourselves. I don't know if I can go back to the way things were before."

Antonio studied him for a moment, his expression unreadable. Finally, he spoke again, his voice softer this time. "The world is complicated, yes. But perhaps it's also simpler than you think. You've always been a dreamer, Thomas. Perhaps it's time for you to share what you've learned with the people here. Your journey can inspire others. You've always wanted to explore the world, but now you've discovered something even more important."

"What's that?" Thomas asked.

Antonio placed a hand on the stack of maps before him, his fingers tracing the edges of one that seemed older than the rest. "Home, Thomas. You've seen the world, but now it's time to share what you've learned. Your journey is just as much about bringing the world home as it is about going out into it."

Thomas felt a rush of realization. The journey had always been about discovery—about seeking new lands and knowledge. But now he understood that part of the journey was also about bringing that knowledge home, sharing it with the people who had been left behind.

As he looked into his father's eyes, he knew that this was not just a return to Venice—it was a return to himself. The lessons he had learned on his travels were meant to be shared, not kept hidden away in the pages of a journal. It was time for Thomas Polo to bring the world home.

Chapter 19: The Wisdom Gained

The days after Thomas's return to Venice felt surreal. After so many years of being away, the streets seemed both familiar and strange, as though the city he once knew so well had shifted in his absence. Thomas's heart raced with both excitement and trepidation. The world he had left behind, the one of cobbled streets and colorful gondolas, felt so small now in comparison to the vast landscapes and cultures he had encountered. But as he walked through Venice's bustling piazzas and narrow alleyways, Thomas couldn't shake the feeling that he was no longer the boy who had first sailed from these docks all those years ago.

Everywhere he looked, Thomas saw change. His childhood friends had grown into young men and women, busy with their own lives. The marketplace, where he had once wandered with wonder, now seemed crowded and noisy. But amidst this wave of change, there was something constant: the great bell towers, the fluttering of pigeons, and the ever-present murmur of the Grand Canal, reminding him that some things in life, like home, never truly change.

One evening, after dinner, Thomas sat in the study of his family home, looking out at the darkening sky. His mother, Lucia, had long since retired for the night, and Antonio, his father, had gone to the docks to oversee the latest shipments of cargo. But Thomas had no desire to sleep. His mind was still spinning with thoughts of his travels, the stories he had gathered, and the many lessons that had shaped his journey.

As he sat there in silence, a faint knock on the door broke his reverie. It was his father, who entered without waiting for a response.

"I've been thinking," Antonio said, sitting down across from Thomas, "about what we discussed the other day."

Thomas looked up from the table, startled. "What do you mean?"

Antonio smiled, his eyes softening as he leaned back in his chair. "When you first came back, you mentioned how much you had learned. About the world. About yourself. Well, I've been reflecting on that, too. And I've come to understand something important."

Thomas waited, unsure of what his father was about to say. Antonio had never been one for sentimental words or grand gestures. But when he spoke, it was always with purpose.

"You've always had the spirit of an adventurer, Thomas," Antonio continued. "But now you've come back a man. A man who has learned the true value of exploration."

Thomas nodded, unsure of where this conversation was heading, but sensing that his father was trying to express something deeper.

"I know I pushed you to stay here in Venice," Antonio said. "To follow in my footsteps. But now I see the truth—you've walked the world. You've seen things that I only dreamt of in my youth. And that has shaped you into someone with a unique perspective. What I didn't realize all those years was that your adventure wasn't just about seeing distant lands. It was about discovering the deeper meaning of what it means to be alive, to connect with people, and to find wisdom in unexpected places."

Thomas felt a pang of emotion at his father's words. He had spent so much of his life seeking his father's approval, but now it seemed like Antonio was seeing him not just as his son, but as a man who had truly become something more.

"Father," Thomas said quietly, "the journey... it was never about the destination. I thought it was. I thought if I could just get to the East, just see China and the Mongol Empire, I would have all the answers. But what I've learned is that the answers don't lie in distant places or grand palaces. They lie in the people we meet, in the moments of silence when we stop to listen, in the small gestures that speak volumes."

Antonio looked at his son, his gaze steady. "That's what your grandfather knew. He always said that it's not enough to travel the world for the sake of adventure. One must return, to share what's been learned, and to leave something behind."

Thomas looked down at his hands, realizing the weight of his father's words. The adventures he had lived, the cultures he had witnessed, and the lessons he had absorbed—they weren't just for him. They were meant to be shared. He had a story to tell, a message to impart.

"I've thought a lot about that," Thomas said. "I want to share what I've learned. Not just about the East, but about the world itself. About the connections between people, and how much we all share despite our differences."

Antonio nodded. "And that's why I'm giving you this."

He reached into his coat and pulled out a small, worn leather book. It was heavy, the kind of book that had seen many years and many hands. Antonio placed it in front of Thomas, who recognized it at once. It was the journal of his grandfather—the same one his father had always kept hidden away in the family's library. A record of voyages, personal reflections, and observations about the places his grandfather had traveled to long before Thomas had even dreamed of sailing.

"This was your grandfather's," Antonio said. "He was a traveler like you, though in a different way. His journey was not just to foreign lands but into the heart of what it means to be human. He believed that to understand the world, one must first understand oneself."

Thomas opened the book, his fingers trembling slightly. The pages were filled with handwritten notes, drawings of unfamiliar places, and sketches of the faces his grandfather had met. But more than the illustrations, it was the words that struck him most. They were filled with wisdom—about patience, about love, about the importance of listening.

"I see now, Father," Thomas said, closing the book with reverence. "What my journey has really been about. It wasn't just about the East, about Marco Polo or Kublai Khan. It was about understanding the human spirit—what unites us, what makes us different, and how we're all connected."

Antonio smiled, a proud and contented look on his face. "Exactly. Your journey wasn't just about traveling to places. It was about learning how to live. To be present in the world, to listen, to understand, and to teach others what you've learned."

Thomas stood up from the chair and walked over to the window, looking out at the familiar sights of Venice. The canals shimmered in the moonlight, the gondolas swaying gently in the water. He had come full circle. The boy who once dreamed of distant lands now understood that his real journey was one of understanding—understanding the world, and understanding himself.

As he looked out over the city he had left behind, Thomas made a decision. He would take everything he had learned, every lesson and every experience, and share them with the world. It was time to write his story—not just of the places he had visited, but of the lessons he had learned, the people he had met, and the wisdom he had gained.

His journey was far from over. In many ways, it had only just begun. And this time, the journey would be about sharing what he had learned with others, inspiring them to follow their own paths and seek their own truths. Because, in the end, Thomas realized, the world wasn't just out there to be explored. It was inside each of us, waiting to be discovered.

Chapter 20: A New Path Forward

The months that followed Thomas's return were filled with a deep sense of purpose. He had no intention of returning to a life of quiet anonymity, tied solely to the docks of Venice. His heart had been reshaped by his travels, his spirit transformed by the experiences that had taken him to places he had never imagined. And now, with his father's blessing and the support of his mother, he was ready to share the knowledge he had gained.

The book, his book, began to take form. Each page was a reflection of the world he had seen—a world full of wonder, challenges, and the rich diversity of human experience. As he sat at his desk each night, Thomas could feel the weight of the stories he was about to tell. He wrote about the people he had met, the landscapes that had stretched beyond his wildest dreams, and the wisdom that had been imparted to him along the way.

At first, the writing came slowly. The memories of distant lands were so vast, so layered, that it was hard to know where to start. Should he begin with the vast desert winds that had howled through his veins as he crossed Persia? Or with the awe he had felt when standing before the majestic walls of the Great Wall of China? Should he recount the quiet nights spent in the Mongol camps, beneath a sky full of stars, listening to tales of empires that stretched across continents?

But as the days passed, the words began to flow more freely. The lessons he had learned about humanity—the value of kindness, the importance of humility, and the beauty of connection—became the foundation of his story. He wrote not just for himself but for the generations that would come after him. He wanted to inspire them to look beyond their familiar surroundings, to see the world with fresh eyes and open hearts.

But writing wasn't the only change Thomas experienced. His relationships with his family grew deeper as well. Antonio, once so distant in his expectations, became a quiet but steadfast source of support. He would often sit with Thomas as he wrote, listening intently to the stories of the East and offering his thoughts. Lucia, his mother, had always been a quiet force in his life, and now her quiet wisdom seemed even more important to him. She encouraged him not only to share his story but to share the lessons that had brought him peace.

One evening, as the sun dipped below the horizon, Thomas walked through the bustling streets of Venice with his father. The warm golden light of the fading day reflected off the water, casting a soft glow on the narrow buildings and cobblestone streets. Antonio had taken Thomas to the Rialto Bridge, a familiar place in the city, but tonight it felt different. The city seemed to hum with possibility.

"You've changed, son," Antonio said quietly, looking out over the water. "When you left, you were a boy with dreams of the unknown. Now, you're a man who understands the value of what's here, as well as what's out there."

Thomas smiled, his eyes looking out over the canal. “I didn’t realize it until I was far from home, Father. But Venice... this city, these people—they are the foundation. Everything I learned out there is only meaningful because of what I came from. I see that now.”

Antonio nodded, his gaze softening. "Your grandfather always said that home is the starting point of every journey. And maybe he was right. But it’s not just about coming home, Thomas. It’s about what you bring back with you."

As the days turned to weeks, Thomas’s book neared completion. He had written about the grandeur of Kublai Khan’s court, the bustling markets of the Silk Road, and the quiet nights spent beneath the stars in the Mongol Empire. He had written about the diverse cultures, the exchange of ideas, and the universal desire for connection. But as he looked over the pages, he realized there was one more chapter he needed to write—a chapter that was more personal than anything else he had written so far.

It was a reflection on himself—on how the journey had changed him, and on how it had helped him understand the world in ways he could never have anticipated. It wasn’t just a book about exploration; it was a book about the inner journey, about how the act of traveling can transform the soul.

Chapter 21: A Legacy for the Future

Years had passed since Thomas Polo’s return to Venice, but the memories of his travels remained as vivid as ever. His book, *The Boy Who Crossed the World with Marco Polo*, had become a beacon of inspiration for many. As the first copies found their way into the hands of eager readers, they spread quickly through the city and beyond, reaching the distant corners of Italy and the East. His words had begun to inspire a new generation of adventurers, thinkers, and dreamers, all longing to follow in his footsteps.

But it was not just the tales of faraway lands or the grandeur of the Mongol Empire that resonated with his readers. It was the deeper truth he had discovered about himself, the essence of what it meant to embark on a journey—not just through the world, but through one's own soul.

Thomas had never intended for his words to become a legacy. At first, he had written for himself—to make sense of the world he had seen, to give meaning to his journey. But now, he realized his words were doing something far greater. They were connecting people, uniting them across vast distances, and reminding them that the world was both a place of adventure and of profound humanity.

Standing once again on the Rialto Bridge, looking out over the familiar waters of the Grand Canal, Thomas could see the reflection of his own transformation. The city that had once felt so small to him now seemed vast with possibility. Venice had always been his home, but now, it was a reminder of where his journey had begun—where he had set out, wide-eyed and uncertain, and where he had returned, changed in ways he could never have predicted.

But even with the success of his book, he knew that his own personal journey was not over. There were still corners of the world he had yet to explore, mysteries he had yet to solve. His travels had taught him that knowledge was not a destination but a continuous journey. It was the same with life itself. To stop exploring was to stop growing.

As he gazed at the setting sun, he thought of the many travelers who had crossed paths with him during his journey. Each one had contributed to his understanding of the world in ways they could never have imagined. The traders in Persia, the monks in China, the sailors on the ship—each person had left an imprint on his soul, each had shared a piece of their world with him. And now, he was passing that knowledge forward, hoping to inspire the same sense of wonder and possibility in others.

His thoughts turned to Marco Polo. The Venetian explorer whose own adventures had once seemed like the stuff of legend. It was Marco's courage, his relentless pursuit of discovery, that had sparked Thomas's desire to explore the world. But now, as Thomas stood at the threshold of his future, he realized something profound: Marco Polo had not simply mapped the world for others; he had opened a door to a future that was still unfolding.

And so, Thomas Polo's journey had become a legacy, not just through his book, but through the lives of those who would follow his example. Young people from Venice and beyond now dreamed of distant lands, of cultures and peoples unknown to them, driven by the same curiosity that had once propelled Thomas across the seas. They saw in his story the truth that exploration was not just about reaching distant places—it was about reaching deep within oneself, about discovering new dimensions of possibility and understanding.

As he walked back toward his home, the sounds of Venice buzzing around him, Thomas felt a sense of peace settle over him. His journey, both outward and inward, had come full circle. He had returned to the place where it all began, but he was no longer the boy who had dreamed of the East from the docks of Venice. He was a man who had seen the world, who had lived its stories, and who now understood that the world itself—no matter how vast or mysterious—was a reflection of the infinite possibilities that existed within each person.

And though his adventures had brought him back to Venice, Thomas knew that his true journey was far from over. The world was still there, waiting for those who dared to seek it.

Chapter 22: The World Awaits

Conclusion

The World Awaits

The journey of Thomas Polo, like all true journeys, was not just about discovering new places but about discovering himself. Through the cities he visited, the cultures he encountered, and the challenges he faced, he learned that the world is both vast and interconnected—no matter how far apart the lands may seem. What he found was that each new experience added depth to his understanding of humanity and to his own heart.

Thomas's story is a reminder to us all that the world is full of wonders, waiting to be discovered. And more importantly, it is a reminder that the greatest journeys are often those that lead us back to ourselves. It's about understanding the meaning behind the footsteps we take and the lessons we learn from the people we meet along the way.

As I write these words, I think of the many people like Thomas who dare to dream of a world beyond their own boundaries, who seek adventure, wisdom, and connection. The legacy of Marco Polo lives on not only through his travels but through all who are inspired by his courage and curiosity.

I, too, have been inspired by this tale of exploration, both in my own life and in my writing. Just as Thomas crossed the world with Marco Polo, we all have our own paths to follow. The journey of life is not about reaching a final destination but about embracing the adventure, learning from the challenges, and living fully in each moment.

To those who read this story, I offer this: the world awaits. No matter where you are, no matter who you are, there is always a new horizon to explore, a new story to tell, and a new discovery to be made. Never stop dreaming, never stop seeking, and most importantly, never stop believing in the power of your own journey.

Also by Fayzullakhuja Uktamboev

Dreamers and Doers: Inspirational Journeys of Legendary Figures
Pawn to King: A Chess Champion's Rise
The Boy Who Crossed the World with Marco Polo
The Boy Who Crossed the World with Marco Polo

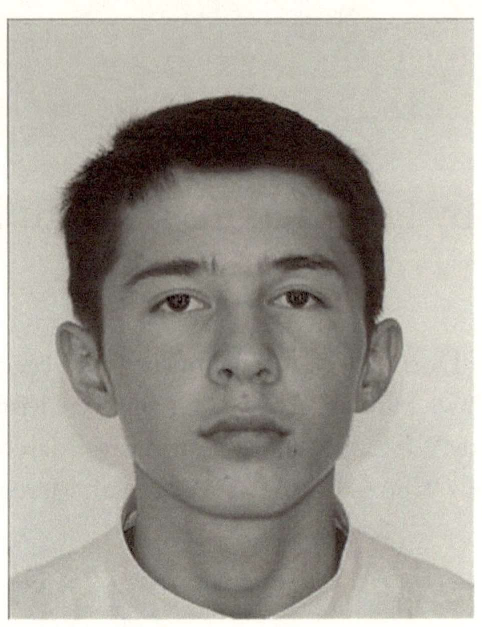

About the Publisher

Uktamboev Fayzullakhuja is an emerging author from Uzbekistan with a passion for sharing inspiring stories and exploring the power of dreams.At just 16 years old , Uktamboev has embarked on a journey to write books that uplift, motivate, and ignite the imagination of readers worldwide.

As a dedicated writer, he blends storytelling with themes of resilience, ambition, and personal growth. His work reflects a unique perspective, drawing from his experiences and aspirations to encourage others to pursue their dreams relentlessly.

Beyond writing, Uktamboev enjoys reading, learning about history, and working towards excellence in academics. His mission is to create stories that leave a lasting impact on young readers and inspire them to dream big and achieve their goals.

Whether through his books or future projects, Uktamboev Fayzullakhuja is a name to watch in the world of inspirational literature.

www.ingramcontent.com/pod-product-compliance
Lightning Source LLC
LaVergne TN
LVHW091123150826
845673LV00002B/945
* 9 7 9 8 2 3 0 6 4 2 0 2 2 *